D1551522

DEEPENING
LIFE
TOGETHER

REVELATION

LIFE TOGETHER

BakerBooks
a division of Baker Publishing Group
Grand Rapids, Michigan

© 2009 by Lifetogether Publishing

Published by Baker Books
a division of Baker Publishing Group
P.O. Box 6287, Grand Rapids, MI 49516-6287
www.bakerbooks.com

Printed in the United States of America

Library of Congress Cataloging-in-Publication Data
Revelation / [editors, Mark L. Strauss, Teresa Haymaker].
    p.   cm. — (Deepening life together)
  ISBN 978-0-8010-6846-1 (pbk.)
    1. Bible. N.T. Revelation—Textbooks. 2. Bible. N.T. Revelation—Study and teaching.
I. Strauss, Mark L. II. Haymaker, Teresa.
BS2825.55.R48 2009
228.0071—dc22   2009014724

CONTENTS

Contents

ACKNOWLEDGMENTS

The *Deepening Life Together: Revelation* Small Group Video Bible Study has come together through the efforts of many at Baker Publishing Group, Lifetogether Publishing, and Lamplighter Media, for which we express our heartfelt thanks.

Executive Producer	John Nill
Producer and Director	Sue Doc Ross
Editors	Mark L. Strauss (Scholar), Teresa Haymaker
Curriculum Development	Brett Eastman, Kathleen Fuller, Craig Keener, Sue Doc Ross, Stephanie French, Teresa Haymaker, Mark L. Strauss, Karen Lee-Thorp
Video Production	Chris Balish, Rodney Bissell, Nick Calabrese, Sebastian Hoppe Fuentes, Josh Greene, Patrick Griffin, Teresa Haymaker, Oziel Jabin Ibarra, Natali Ibarra, Janae Janik, Keith Sorrell, Lance Tracy
Teachers and Scholars	Ray Bentley, Scott Duvall, Andrew Hill, Alan Hultberg, Craig Keener, Jon Laansma, Nick Perrin, Mark Strauss, David Talley
Baker Publishing Group	Jack Kuhatschek

Special thanks to DeLisa Ivy, Bethel Seminary, Talbot School of Theology, Wheaton College

Interior icons by Tom Clark

READ ME FIRST

Most people want to live a healthy, balanced spiritual life, but few achieve this by themselves. And most small groups struggle to balance all of God's purposes in their meetings. Groups tend to overemphasize one of the five purposes, perhaps fellowship or discipleship. Rarely is there a healthy balance that includes evangelism, ministry, and worship. That's why we've included all of these elements in this study so you can live a healthy, balanced spiritual life over time.

A typical group session will include the following:

Memory Verses

For each session we have provided a memory verse that emphasizes an important truth from the session. This is an optional exercise, but we believe that memorizing Scripture can be a vital part of filling our minds with God's Word. We encourage you to give this important habit a try.

 CONNECTING *with God's Family (Fellowship)*

The foundation for spiritual growth is an intimate connection with God and his family. A few people who really know you and who earn your trust provide a place to experience the life Jesus invites you to live. This section of each session typically offers you two activities. You can get to know your whole group by using the icebreaker question, and/or you can check in with one or two group members—your spiritual partner(s)—for a deeper connection and encouragement in your spiritual journey.

DVD TEACHING SEGMENT. A *Deepening Life Together: Revelation* Video Teaching DVD companion to this study guide is available. For each study session, the DVD contains a lesson taught by Ray Bentley. If you are using the DVD, you will view the teaching segment after your *Connecting* discussion and before your group discussion time (the *Growing* section). At the end of each session in this study guide you will find space for your notes on the teaching segment.

GROWING *to Be Like Christ* (*Discipleship*)

Here is where you come face-to-face with Scripture. In core passages you'll explore what the Bible teaches about the topic of the study. The focus won't be on accumulating information but on how we should live in light of the Word of God. We want to help you apply the Scriptures practically, creatively, and from your heart as well as your head. At the end of the day, allowing the timeless truths from God's Word to transform our lives in Christ is our greatest aim.

DEVELOPING *Your Gifts to Serve Others* (*Ministry*)

Jesus trained his disciples to discover and develop their gifts to serve others. And God has designed each of us uniquely to serve him in a way no other person can. This section will help you discover and use your God-given design. It will also encourage your group to discover your unique design as a community. In this study, you'll put into practice what you've learned in the Bible study by taking a step to serve others. These simple steps will take your group on a faith journey that could change your lives forever.

SHARING *Your Life Mission Every Day (Evangelism)*

Many people skip over this aspect of the Christian life because it's scary, relationally awkward, or simply too much work for their busy schedules. But Jesus wanted all of his disciples to help outsiders connect with him, to know him personally. This doesn't mean preaching on street corners. It could mean welcoming a few newcomers into your group, hosting a short-term group in your home, or walking through this study with a friend. In this study, you'll have an opportunity to go beyond Bible study to biblical living.

SURRENDERING *Your Life for God's Pleasure (Worship)*

God is most pleased by a heart that is fully his. Each group session will give you a chance to surrender your heart to God in prayer and worship. You may read a psalm together, share a page in your journal, or sing a song to close your meeting. If you have never prayed aloud in a group before, no one will pressure you. Instead, you'll experience the support of others who are praying for you.

Study Notes

This section provides background notes on the Bible passage(s) you examine in the *Growing* section. You may want to refer to these notes during your group meeting or as a reference for those doing additional study.

For Deeper Study (Optional)

If you want to dig deeper into more Bible passages about the topic at hand, we've provided additional passages and questions. Your group may choose to do study homework ahead of each meeting in order to cover more biblical material. Or you as an individual may choose to study the *For Deeper Study* on your own. If you prefer not to do study homework, the *Growing* section will provide you with plenty to discuss within the group. These options allow individuals or the whole group to go deeper in their study, while still accommodating those who can't do homework or are new to your group.

You can record your discoveries in your journal. We encourage you to read some of your insights to a friend (spiritual partner) for accountability and support. Spiritual partners may check in each week over the phone, through e-mail, or at the beginning of the group meeting.

Reflections

On the *Reflections* pages we provide Scriptures to read and reflect on between group meetings. We suggest you use this section to seek God at home throughout the week. This time at home should begin and end with prayer. Don't get in a hurry; take enough time to hear God's direction.

Subgroup for Discussion and Prayer

If your group is large (more than seven people), we encourage you to separate into groups of two to four for discussion and prayer. This is to encourage greater participation and deeper discussion.

INTRODUCTION

Welcome to the *Deepening Life Together* Bible study on the book of *Revelation*. You are about to embark on journey into understanding God's wondrous plan of redemption for the world. We will take you step-by-step through Jesus's revelation to the apostle John—the vision of God's throne room, the Lord's judgment of humanity, and the hope we can all share because of God's abundant mercy. What you will discover as you study through this final book of the Bible will inspire, encourage, and edify your faith, in addition to strengthening your life's journey with the Lord.

For some of you, this might be the first time you've connected in a small group community. We want to encourage you that God cares about you and your spiritual growth. As you respond to the principles you learn, God will empower your growth. Approach this study prayerfully and God will move you to a deeper level of commitment and intimacy with himself, as well as with those in your small group.

This journey of discovery will make known God's purposes for our lives. We will connect with our loving and faithful God and with other believers in small group community. We will become his hands and feet here on earth as he reveals our uniqueness and his willingness to use us. We will experience the closeness that he desires with us as we prayerfully respond to the principles we learn in this study and learn to place him first in our lives.

We at Baker Books and Lifetogether Publishing look forward to hearing the stories of how God changes you from the inside out during this small group experience. We pray God blesses you with all he has planned for you through this journey together.

For the LORD is good and his love endures forever;
his faithfulness continues through all generations.

Psalm 100:5 (NIV)

SESSION ONE

SETTING
AUDIENCE AND THE REVEALER

Memory Verse: "I am the Alpha and the Omega," says the Lord God, "who is, and who was, and who is to come, the Almighty" (Rev. 1:8).

Anne loved her Nana's visits. Nana lived in a different state, but she came to visit at least once a year. From the moment she learned of Nana's impending arrival, Anne would impatiently count down the days with eagerness and anticipation. On the appointed day, she and her parents would go to the airport together to greet Nana. The minutes would drag on like months as she pressed her nose against the cold pane of the air terminal glass, searching for signs of the plane.

When Anne saw the lights blinking in the distance and heard the rumble of the engine, excitement tingled through her. As the passengers disembarked, Anne would watch them pass by, one by one, looking for her fair-haired Nana. Eventually she would emerge, and Anne would run toward her, thrilled to see her again and receive one of her wonderful hugs.

Christians are also anticipating a special and important arrival. While the apostle John was exiled on the island of Patmos, Jesus

13

revealed to him the circumstances surrounding his return to earth. Although we don't know the exact time when our Savior will come again, we do know that he will return and "every eye will see him." Jesus told John of his redemptive plan for his people and for creation. It is a plan we can all look forward to.

Connecting

Prayer is a powerful way to connect as a group. Open your group with prayer and invite the Holy Spirit to lead you as you begin your study in the book of *Revelation*.

Deeper relationships happen when we take the time to keep in touch with one another between sessions. As you begin, pass around a copy of the *Small Group Roster*, a sheet of paper, or one of you pass your study guide, opened to the *Small Group Roster*. When the roster gets to you write down your contact information, including the best time and method for contacting you. Then, someone volunteer to make copies or type up a list with everyone's information and e-mail it to the group this week.

1. Begin this first session by introducing yourselves. Include your name, what you do for a living, and what you do for fun. You may also include whether or not you are married/how long you have been married, how many children you have, and their ages.

2. Whether your group is new or ongoing, it's always important to reflect on and review your values together. In the *Appendix* is a *Small Group Agreement* with the values most useful in developing and sustaining healthy, balanced small groups. Choose two or three values that you haven't previously focused on, or have room to grow in, to emphasize during this study. Choose values that will take your group to the next stage of intimacy and spiritual health.

If your group is new, you may want to focus on welcoming newcomers or on sharing group ownership. Any group will quickly move from being *the leader's group* to *our group* if everyone understands the goals of the group and shares a small role. See the *Team Roles* in the *Appendix* for help on how to do this well.

3. Share your expectations for the study. How do you hope God will challenge you?

Growing

In the first chapter of Revelation, John is in exile on the island of Patmos when he receives a vision from Jesus (see the *Study Notes* for more information on Patmos). John is directed to address the churches in Asia (see the *Study Notes* for more information on the churches) who are in various states of obedience, compromise, and persecution. Even though John's audience is those churches in particular, he gives this message to all readers: "Blessed is the one who reads the words of this prophecy, and blessed are those who hear it and take to heart what is written in it, because the time is near" (Rev. 1:3 NIV).

Take turns reading through Revelation 1 aloud.

4. Who is giving the revelation (1:1)? Why does this matter?

   What is the purpose of the revelation (1:1–2)?

5. John is in exile on the island of Patmos when he receives this revelation. What does verse 1:9 say about John and why he is on the island?

   What is significant to you about the way John chooses to describe himself and the Christian life as he experiences it?

6. When John hears the Lord's voice he is "in the Spirit" (v. 10)? What do you think it means to be "in the Spirit"?

15

7. John writes to seven churches in the Roman province of Asia (present day western Turkey). He first sees the glorified Christ (vv. 13–16). Review the chart below and discuss what these aspects of his appearance say about Jesus after his resurrection.

Jesus's Appearance	Symbolism
Robe—full length with a golden sash (v. 13)	Jesus is the High Priest
Hair like white wool, like snow (v. 14)	Wisdom
Eyes like fire (v. 14)	Deep insight, judgment over evil
Feet like bronze glowing in a furnace (v. 15)	Power, victory
Voice like the sound of rushing waters (v. 15)	Authority
Right hand holds seven stars (v. 16)	Protection, control
Double-edged sword comes from his mouth (v. 16)	Power and force of his judgment
Face brilliant like the sun (v. 16)	Christ's glory

How do you respond to this picture of Christ? For instance, is this someone you feel drawn to worship? Obey? Back away from?

8. Note how John reacts to meeting the glorified Jesus (v. 17). In your own words, what is Jesus saying about himself in verses 17–19?

What is John instructed to write (v. 19; see also vv. 1–2)?

9. To whom does 1:3 offer a blessing?

What do you think is the significance of this promise? (See the *Study Notes* for insight into the prophecy and what it means to be "blessed.")

"The time is near" (v. 3). What do you think this means? See
Matthew 24:36–39 and 2 Peter 3:3–10 for help.

John is allowed to witness Jesus in his glorified state. Jesus appears
to him and instructs him to record Jesus's message for posterity.
Throughout chapter 1, John is reassured by Jesus's assertions of
his sovereignty and power. As our study in Revelation continues, we
will discover what awaits humanity and how believers can find hope
through God's plan of redemption.

Developing

Jesus used John to communicate God's plan of redemption to the
world. John took his role as God's servant seriously. We too are
God's servants, and we are called to use our gifts and talents to
serve his kingdom.

10. Developing our ability to serve God according to the leading
    of the Holy Spirit requires that we make time to let God speak
    to us daily. Which of the following next steps toward this goal
    are you willing to take for the next few weeks?

    ☐ *Prayer.* Commit to daily time in personal, focused prayer
    and connection with God. Find a place where you can be
    alone and undistracted. You may find it helpful to write
    your prayers in a journal.

    ☐ *Reflection.* At the end of each session you'll find *Reflec-
    tions*—Scriptures that specifically relate to the topic of our
    study each week. These are provided to give you an oppor-
    tunity for reading a short Bible passage five days a week
    during the course of this study. Write down your insights
    on what you read each day in the space provided. On the
    sixth day, summarize what God has shown you throughout
    the week.

    ☐ *Meditation.* Meditation is focused attention on the Word of
    God—a great way to internalize God's Word more deeply.
    Copy a portion of Scripture on a card and tape it some-

where in your line of sight, such as your car's dashboard, the bathroom mirror, or the kitchen table. Think about it when you sit at red lights, while you get ready for your day, or while you're eating a meal. Reflect on what God is saying to you through these words. Consider using the *memory verse* and *Reflections* verses provided each week for meditation.

Sharing

Jesus commissioned all of his disciples to be his witnesses in Acts 1:8: "You will receive power when the Holy Spirit comes on you; and you will be my witnesses in Jerusalem, and in all Judea and Samaria, and to the ends of the earth" (NIV). We become witnesses through our everyday lives. But he does not expect us to do it alone; the Holy Spirit will empower us to confidently serve and share him with others as we trust in him.

11. In the weeks to come, you'll be asked to identify and share with people in your circle of influence who need to know Jesus or need to connect with him through a small group community. With this in mind, as you go about your day-to-day activities this week, pay special attention to the people God has placed in your life. There may be co-workers, family or friends, or other parents at school or sporting events that you see or talk to on a regular basis. When we meet next week, we'll talk about how we can begin sharing Jesus with those who don't yet know him as well as how to help connect believers to Christian community.

Surrendering

John was "in the Spirit" when he received Jesus's revelation. Just like John, we must surrender ourselves to the Lord in order to do his will. This can be accomplished through dedicated prayer and worship.

12. Every believer should have a plan for spending time alone with God. Your time with God is personal and reflects who you are in relationship with God. However you choose to spend your time with him, try to allow time for praise, prayer, and reading of Scripture. *Reflections* are provided at the end of each session for you to use as part of your daily time with him. These will offer reinforcement of the principles we are learning, and develop or strengthen your habit of time alone with God throughout the week.

13. Before you close your group in prayer, allow everyone to answer this question: "How can we pray for you this week?" Write prayer requests on your *Prayer and Praise Report* and commit to praying for each other throughout the week.

Study Notes

Blessed: Blessed here means spiritually favored, fortunate, well off.

Patmos: A small (four by eight miles), rocky island in the Aegean Sea, about 50 miles southwest of Ephesus, off the coast of modern day Turkey.

Prophecy: Revelation is a book of prophecy that is both prediction (foretelling future events) and proclamation (preaching about who God is and what he will do). Behind the predictions are important principles about God's character and promises.

Seven: Nearly two-thirds of the uses of seven in the New Testament are symbolic uses found in Revelation. The symbolism conveys the message that both judgment and salvation are complete, or at least will be in the final consummation. It is used to describe lampstands (Rev. 1:12), stars (1:16), angels (1:20), spirits of God (3:1), seals (5:1), trumpets (8:2), heads of a dragon (12:3), plagues (15:1), etc.

Seven Churches: These churches formed a circle in Asia, a Roman province lying in present day Turkey. The churches were possibly the postal centers of the seven geographic regions in the area.

Reflections

Reading, reflecting, and meditating on the Word of God is essential to getting to know him deeply. As you read the verses each day, give prayerful consideration to what you learn about God, his Spirit, and his place in your life. Then record your thoughts, insights, or prayer in the *Reflect* section below the verses you read. On the sixth day, record a summary of what you learned over the entire week through this study.

Day 1. The Revelation of Jesus Christ, which God gave him to show his servants what must soon take place (Rev. 1:1 NIV).

REFLECT

_____

_____

_____

_____

Day 2. Blessed is the one who reads the words of this prophecy, and blessed are those who hear it and take to heart what is written in it, because the time is near (Rev. 1:3 NIV).

REFLECT

_____

_____

_____

_____

Day 3. From Jesus Christ, who is the faithful witness, the first-born from the dead, and ruler of the kings of the earth (Rev. 1:5 NIV).

REFLECT

_____

_____

_____

_____

Day 4. To him who loves us, and had freed us from our sins by his blood, and has made us to be a kingdom and priests to serve his God and Father—to him be glory and power forever and ever! (Rev. 1:5–6 NIV).

REFLECT

_____

_____

_____

_____

Day 5. Do not be afraid. I am the First and the Last. I am the Living One; I was dead, and behold I am alive for ever and ever! And I hold the keys of death and Hades (Rev. 1:17–18 NIV).

REFLECT

_____

_____

_____

_____

***Day* 6.** Use the following space to write any thoughts God has put in your heart and mind about the things we have looked at in this session and during your *Reflections* time this week.

SUMMARY

_____

_____

_____

_____

SUFFERING BELIEVERS

Memory Verse: Since you have kept my command to endure patiently, I will also keep you from the hour of trial that is going to come upon the whole world to test those who live on the earth (Rev. 3:10 NIV).

A man loyal to the Lord, Job had everything—a loving family, a prosperous business, and many good friends. Satan challenged Job's faith in God, contending that Job's faith was so strong because everything in his life was perfect. God allowed Satan to do his worst to Job, knowing all along that Job's faith would withstand the testing. In the face of such horrible events as losing his family, the betrayal of his friends, and painful physical illness, Job maintained his devotion to God. In the end God restored Job—his righteousness rewarded. Thankfully, believers will be rewarded with God's promised eternal life, and the victor's crown as well, when we endure in the face of trials and testing.

Revelation

Connecting

Open your group with prayer. Ask God to challenge you in a new way through today's session.

1. If you have new people joining you for the first time, take a few minutes to briefly introduce yourselves.

2. Healthy small groups *rotate leadership*. We recommend that you rotate leaders on a regular basis. This practice helps to develop every member's ability to shepherd a few people within a safe environment. Even Jesus gave others the opportunity to serve alongside him (Mark 6:30–44).

   It's also a good idea to *rotate host homes*, with the host of each meeting providing the refreshments. Some groups like to let the host lead the meeting each week, while others like to allow one person host while another person leads.

   The *Small Group Calendar* is a tool for planning who will lead and host each meeting. Take a few minutes to plan leaders and hosts for your remaining meetings. Don't pass up this opportunity! It will revolutionize your group.

   For information on leading your group, see the *Leader's Notes* introduction in the *Appendix*. Also, if you are leading for the first time, see *Leading for the First Time (Leadership 101)* in the *Appendix*. If you still have questions about rotating hosts and/or homes, refer to the *Frequently Asked Questions (FAQs)* in the *Appendix*.

3. If you had five days left on earth, what three things would you do?

Growing

Two of the churches Jesus addressed in Revelation were Smyrna and Philadelphia. The letters to these churches reveal suffering churches trying to persevere in the face of trials and testing.

Read Revelation 2:8–11 and 3:7–13. Refer to the chart below and discuss the questions that follow.

	Smyrna (Rev. 2:8–11)	Philadelphia (Rev. 3:7–8, 10, 12)
Character of Jesus Revealed	These are the words of him who is the First and the Last, who died and came to life again (v. 8).	These are the words of him who is holy and true, who holds the key of David. What he opens no one can shut and what he shuts no one can open (v. 7).
Commendations for the Church	I know your afflictions and your poverty—yet you are rich! (v. 9a).	I know that you have little strength, yet you have kept my word and have not denied my name (v. 8).
Challenges Ahead for the Church	I know the slander of those who say they are Jews and are not, but are a synagogue of Satan. I tell you, the devil will put some of you in prison to test you, and you will suffer persecution for ten days (vv. 9b–10).	I will also keep you from the hour of trial that is going to come upon the whole world to test those who live on the earth (v. 10).
Promises for Those Who Endure	He who overcomes will not be hurt at all by the second death (v. 11).	Him who overcomes I will make a pillar in the temple of my God (v. 12).

4. In your own words, what do 2:8 and 3:7 reveal about Jesus?

   How do these things matter to you?

5. Look at the commendations Jesus offers to the churches at Smyrna (2:9a) and Philadelphia (3:8). Could Jesus say these things about you? Please explain.

6. How are the challenges facing these churches (2:9b–10; 3:10) like challenges facing some Christian communities today?

7. How would you explain in your own words the promises Jesus makes for those who endure?

25

8. Read through Revelation 2:8–11 and 3:7–13 again. Note the occurrences of the word "I" as Jesus speaks to each church. What do you think is the significance of Jesus's use of "I" in these verses?

9. What will you take away from Jesus's message to these two churches?

Jesus reassures the churches of Smyrna and Philadelphia by telling them that he knows what they have done in his name and the suffering they have endured. He gives the believers in these churches comfort and hope for those who endure.

 Developing

One way that we can ensure that the way we live our lives agrees with the faith we profess is through spiritual accountability. Opening our lives to someone and making ourselves vulnerable to their loving admonition could perhaps be one of the most difficult things we do but could result in the deepest and most lasting spiritual growth we've known.

10. Scripture tells us in Ephesians 4:25: "Speak truth each one of you with his neighbor, for we are members of one another" (NASB). With this in mind, take a moment to pair up with someone in your group to be your spiritual partner for the remaining weeks of this study (men partner with men and women with women). Once you have done this, turn to the *Personal Health Plan.*

In the box that says, "WHO are you connecting with spiritually?" write your partner's name. In the box that says, "WHAT is your next step for growth?" write one step you would like to take for growth during this study. Tell your partner what step you chose. When you check in with your partner each week, the "Partner's Progress" column on this chart will provide a place to record your partner's progress in the goal he or she chose.

11. Spending time getting to know each other outside of group meetings is helpful to building stronger relationships within your group. Discuss whether your group would like to have a potluck or other type of social to celebrate together what God is doing in your group. You could plan to share a meal prior to a small group meeting or plan to follow your completion of this study with a barbecue. Appoint one or two people who can follow up with everyone outside of group time to put a plan together.

Sharing

Fellowship was a very important aspect of life in the early church. Caring for and sharing with others aren't optional activities—they should be a major part of Christian life.

12. Take a look at the *Circles of Life* diagram below and write the names of two or three people in each circle who you come in contact with on a regular basis who need to be connected in Christian community.

    The people who fill these circles are not there by accident. God has strategically placed each of them within your sphere of influence because he has equipped you to minister to them and share with them in ways no one else can. Consider the following ideas for reaching out to one or two of the people you listed and make a plan to follow through with them this week.

    ☐ This is a wonderful time to welcome a few friends into your group. Which of the people you listed could you invite? It's possible that you may need to help your friend overcome obstacles to coming to a place where he or she can encounter Jesus. Does your friend need a ride to the group or help with childcare?

    ☐ Consider inviting a friend to attend a weekend church service with you and possibly plan to enjoy a meal together

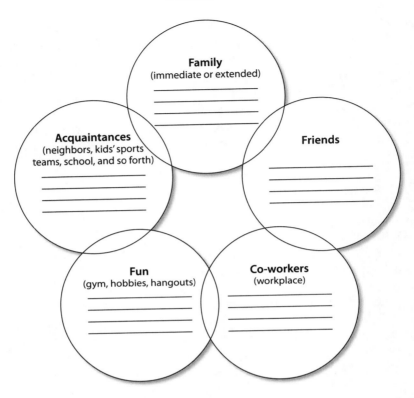

afterward. This can be a great opportunity to talk with someone about your faith in Jesus.

☐ Is there someone who is unable to attend your group but who still needs a connection? Would you be willing to have lunch or coffee with that person, catch up on life, and share something you've learned from this study? Jesus doesn't call all of us to lead small groups, but he does call every disciple to spiritually multiply his or her life over time.

 ## Surrendering

As we discovered in today's study, the Christians of Smyrna and Philadelphia experienced persecution and opposition. This type of oppression could only be overcome by total surrender to the Lord.

13. Share your prayer requests in your group and then gather in smaller circles of three or four people to pray. Be sure to have everyone write down the personal requests of the members to use as a reminder to pray for your group throughout the week. Don't put pressure on anyone to pray aloud. When you pray for each person, you may find it meaningful to hold hands or place your hands on another person's shoulder. Jesus often touched people to communicate his care for them.

14. Take a few minutes to talk about what it would take to make time with God a priority every day or even five or six days a week. Don't put time demands on yourself at first; just make it a priority to draw near to God for a few minutes each day and gradually you will desire more. Use the *Reflections* at the end of each session as a starting point.

Study Notes

Crown of Life: This probably does not refer to an actual crown, but to the victory and reward of eternal life.

New Jerusalem: The future dwelling place of all believers.

Second Death: The "second death" (Rev. 2:11) is the everlasting ruin of the wicked (Rev. 21:8), and "second" in respect to natural or temporal death.

The Synagogue of Satan: A stark metaphor directed against unbelieving, hostile Jews. The synagogue was the worship and gathering place of the Jewish people. Adapted from the *NIV Study Bible* (Zondervan, 1985).

Tribulation: Tribulation is trouble or affliction of any kind, especially the sufferings that will overtake the wicked under the cruel reign of the "beast coming up out of the sea" (Rev. 13:1 NASB) who will command divine worship (Rev. 13:12). The bowl judgments of Revelation 16 are Jesus's final demonstration of power when he destroys his enemies and frees his redeemed from the domination of the wicked at his glorious return.

For Deeper Study (Optional)

Several books of the Bible reference the message of Revelation, particularly "the Day of the Lord" or "the Day of Wrath." Look up the following verses and identify how "the Day of God" is described in each one.

Zephaniah 1:7
Hosea 3:5
Malachi 3:3
Micah 4:1

Reflections

Hopefully last week you made a commitment to read, reflect, and meditate on the Word of God each day. Following are selections of Scripture provided as a starting point to drawing near to God through time with him. Read the daily verses and then record your thoughts, insights, or prayers in the space provided. On the sixth day, record a summary of what you have learned over the entire week through this study or use this space to write down how God has challenged you personally.

Day 1. You have persevered and have endured hardships for my name, and have not grown weary (Rev. 2:3 NIV).

REFLECT

_____
_____
_____
_____

Day 2. Remember the height from which you have fallen! Repent and do the things you did at first (Rev. 2:5 NIV).

REFLECT

_____
_____
_____
_____

Day 3. To him who overcomes, I will give the right to eat from the tree of life, which is in the paradise of God (Rev. 2:7 NIV).

REFLECT

_____
_____
_____
_____

Day 4. He who overcomes will not be hurt at all by the second death (Rev. 2:11 NIV).

REFLECT

_____
_____
_____
_____

Day 5. To him who overcomes, I will give some of the hidden manna. I will also give him a white stone with a new name written on it, known only to him who receives it (Rev. 2:17 NIV).

REFLECT

_____

_____

_____

_____

Day 6. Use this space to record insights, thoughts, or prayers that God has given you during *Session Two* and your *Reflections* time.

SUMMARY

_____

_____

_____

_____

COMPROMISING CHURCHES

Memory Verse: Here I am! I stand at the door and knock. If anyone hears my voice and opens the door, I will come in and eat with him, and he with me (Rev. 3:20 NIV).

God bestowed many blessings on King Solomon, including wealth, wisdom, and prosperity. For years Solomon was faithful to God. He was charged with the important task of building the temple, the sacred place where the Israelites worshiped the Lord. He also built a magnificent palace using the finest craftsmen available. Because of Solomon's devotion to God, the Lord promised to keep Solomon's royal legacy alive. God's only condition was that Solomon had to be faithful to him. If Solomon didn't compromise, God would continue to bless him and his descendants.

However, Solomon didn't fulfill his end of the bargain. He married women from foreign countries, women who worshiped pagan gods. God had warned Solomon not to intermarry, but Solomon ignored his command. As a result, he compromised his faith. Solomon's compromise nullified his agreement with God, and shortly after his reign, Israel plunged into turmoil and was eventually conquered.

Through his actions, Solomon compromised all that God had promised him for the sake of his own desires. Our study this session will reveal how the churches at Pergamum, Thyatira, Sardis, and Laodicea were warned in the book of Revelation of the dangers of unfaithfulness.

Connecting

Open your group with prayer. It can be easy to let prayer become routine or ritualistic. Let's be careful to not just go through the motions but to truly come before God together as we begin this study.

1. Most people want to live a healthy, balanced life. A regular medical check-up is a good way to measure health and spot potential problems. In the same way, a spiritual check-up is vital to your spiritual well-being. The *Personal Health Assessment* was designed to give you a quick snapshot, or pulse, of your spiritual health. Take a few minutes individually to complete the *Personal Health Assessment*, found in the *Appendix*. After answering each question, tally your results.

2. Pair up with your spiritual partner and briefly share one purpose area from your *Personal Health Assessment* where you are strong and one that needs a little work. Share one step you would like to take this week to work on your spiritual health. Note this on your *Personal Health Plan*. Make a note about your partner's plans and how you can pray for him or her this week.

3. Imagine a friend is going through a crisis of faith. How would you help him or her?

Growing

Jesus addresses four more churches in Revelation 2–3: Pergamum is the ancient capital of Asia and is the origin of the English word, "parchment." Thyatira is a military outpost known for having many trade guilds. Sardis is a city of great wealth and fame. Laodicea is another wealthy city with banks, a medical school, and a textile industry. These churches are compromising their beliefs, and Jesus points out this error throughout these verses.

Read Revelation 2:12–3:6 and 3:14–22.

4. What impression do you get of the resurrected Lord from these passages? Look at the table below for the meanings of the way Jesus is described.

Characterization	Meaning
Sharp, double-edged sword (2:12)	Judgment
Eyes blazing fire (2:18)	Discernment
Feet burnished bronze (2:18)	Strength
Words of the One who holds the seven spirits of God (3:1)	Perfection
Words of the Amen, etc. (3:14)	Certainty, veracity

5. Jesus commends the churches for their successes, points out their compromising ways, and warns them about the dangers of unfaithfulness.

	Pergamum (2:12–17)	Thyatira (2:18–29)	Sardis (3:1–6)	Laodicea (3:14–22)
Commen-dations	You did not renounce your faith in me (2:13).	Your love and faith, your service and perseverance, and that you are now doing more than you did at first (2:19).	You have a few people . . . who have not soiled their clothes (3:4).	

	Pergamum (2:12–17)	Thyatira (2:18–29)	Sardis (3:1–6)	Laodicea (3:14–22)
Compromises	You have people there who hold to the teaching of Balaam . . . (2:14, see *Study Notes*). You have those who hold to the teaching of the Nicolaitans (2:15, see *Study Notes*).	You tolerate the woman Jezebel . . . she misleads my servants into sexual immorality and the eating of food sacrificed to idols (2:20).	You have a reputation of being alive, but you are dead. I have not found your deeds complete in the sight of my God (3:1–2).	You are neither cold nor hot (3:15). You do not realize that you are wretched, pitiful, poor, blind and naked (3:17).
Warnings	Repent. . . . Otherwise I will soon come to you and will fight against them with the sword of my mouth (2:16).	I will cast her on a bed of suffering, and I will make those who commit adultery with her suffer intensely, unless they repent of her ways (2:22, see *Study Notes*).	Remember . . . what you have received and heard; obey it, and repent (3:3).	Those whom I love I rebuke and discipline. So be earnest, and repent (3:19).

What are these churches' good qualities?

In your own words, what kinds of compromises are these churches making?

In your own words, what does Jesus want them to do, and what will happen if they don't?

6. In the most forceful terms, Jesus tells all three churches to repent. What do you think we should learn from this repetition?

7. Jesus addresses the invitation of 3:20 to believers. What does Jesus mean when he says these words to believers?

What significance does this verse have for you?

8. What effect do Jesus's forceful words in these passages have on you?

In 3:15 Jesus says, "I know your deeds, that you are neither cold nor hot. I wish you were either one or the other!" (NIV). Being lukewarm in our beliefs isn't what Jesus wants or expects of us. We must be totally devoted to him and uncompromising in our faith in order to receive the reward God has promised us.

Developing

The four churches we studied today received stern warnings from the Lord. There were members of these churches who had gone astray. It is our duty as Christians to keep each other accountable and to help each other when we stumble. Serving others is one way we can interact with our fellow Christians—and make sure we do not fall away from God.

9. Discuss some of the many ways that we can serve the body of Christ. Is there a particular area of service that God has put on your heart to serve either this group or in your local church? If not, investigate the opportunities and pray about finding a ministry in which you can serve. As you take that first step, God will lead you to the ministry that expresses your passion.

Sharing

In his address to the Laodicean church, Jesus describes himself as *the faithful and true witness* (3:14). We are called to be witnesses in our families, our communities, and in the world.

10. In the last session you were asked to write some names in the *Circles of Life* diagram. Have you followed up with those you identified who need to connect with other Christians? If not, when will you contact them? Go back to the *Circles of Life* diagram to remind yourself of the various people you come into contact with on a regular basis.

11. Jesus desires to enter each of our lives in a dramatic and life-changing way. If you have never invited Jesus to take control of your life, why not ask him now? If you are not clear about God's gift of eternal life for everyone who believes in Jesus and how to receive this gift, take a minute to pray and ask God to help you understand what he wants you to do about trusting in Jesus.

Surrendering

Jesus accuses the church in Laodicea of being "lukewarm." God does not want us to have a tepid faith; he wants us to be on fire for him. Total surrender to the Lord is how we can accomplish this.

12. Have one person close this session in prayer, making sure to thank God for all he's done in and through your group to this point.

Study Notes

Antipas: The first martyr of the Roman province of Asia. According to tradition he was slowly roasted to death in a bronze kettle during the reign of the emperor Domitian.

Hot and Cold: "Cold" is sometimes construed to mean standing against God. However, this is not the case, since both "hot" and "cold" were positive images in John's time. "Hot" referred to soothing hot water springs and "cold" referred to fresh mountain water.

Jezebel: A prominent woman in the church who had promoted tolerance toward pagan practices. She is named for the wicked Old Testament queen who opposed the prophet Elijah (1 Kings 18–21).

Nicolaitans: A heretical sect within the church that had worked out a compromise with the pagan society. They apparently taught that spiritual liberty gave them sufficient leeway to practice idolatry and immorality.

Teaching of Balaam: He taught the Midianite women how to lead the Israelite men astray, and is an example of teachers who deceive believers.

For Deeper Study (Optional)

In *Session Two* we looked at several verses from the Old Testament that spoke of Jesus's, return. Here are four more. Look up the following verses and identify how "the Day of God" is described in each one.

Micah 5:10
Obadiah 1:15
Joel 3:14
Isaiah 2:18

Reflections

If you've been spending time each day connecting with God through his Word, congratulations! Some experts say that it takes 21 repetitions to develop a new habit. By the end of this week, you'll be well on your way to cultivating new spiritual habits that will encourage you in your walk with God. This week, continue to read the daily verses, giving prayerful consideration to what you learn about God, his Spirit, and his place in your life. Then, as before, record your thoughts, insights, or prayers in the space provided. On the sixth day, record a summary of what you have learned throughout the week.

Day 1. To him who overcomes and does my will to the end I will give authority over the nations—"He will rule them with an iron scepter; he will dash them to pieces like pottery"—just as I have received authority from my Father. I will also give him the morning star (Rev. 2:26–28 NIV).

REFLECT

_____

_____

_____

_____

Day 2. He who overcomes will, like them, be dressed in white. I will never blot out his name from the book of life, but will acknowledge his name before my Father and his angels (Rev. 3:5 NIV).

REFLECT

_____

_____

_____

_____

Day 3. Him who overcomes I will make a pillar in the temple of my God. Never again will he leave it. I will write on him the name of my God and the name of the city of my God, the new Jerusalem, which is coming down out of heaven from my God; and I will also write on him my new name (Rev. 3:12 NIV).

REFLECT

_____

_____

_____

_____

Day 4. To him who overcomes, I will give the right to sit with me on my throne, just as I overcame and sat down with my Father on his throne (Rev. 3:21 NIV).

REFLECT

_____
_____
_____
_____

Day 5. You are worthy, our Lord and God, to receive glory and honor and power, for you created all things, and by your will they were created and have their being (Rev. 4:11 NIV).

REFLECT

_____
_____
_____
_____

Day 6. Record your weekly summary of what God has shown you in the space below.

SUMMARY

_____
_____
_____
_____

WORSHIP IN HEAVEN

Memory Verse: Holy, holy, holy is the Lord God, the Almighty, who was and
who is and who is to come (Rev. 4:8b NASB).

The Wizard of Oz is a delightful movie. While the characters of Dorothy, the Scarecrow, the Tin Man, and the Lion are great, they aren't the best part of the movie. The part of the film most noteworthy is when Dorothy enters the Land of Oz and follows the yellow brick road. She emerges from the gray, dusty, dreary landscape of Kansas into a world filled with color and light. When she approaches the magnificent Emerald City, she can see its dazzling silhouette in the distance, and she is filled with hope.

In Revelation John describes the images he saw of heaven, images so intense in their grandeur and scope we can barely wrap our minds around them. John sees the splendor awaiting believers who persevere in their faith. Like Dorothy, we too are filled with hope.

 Connecting

Open your group with prayer and invite the Holy Spirit to guide you as you participate in this session.

1. Check in with your spiritual partner(s), or with another partner if yours is absent. Turn to your *Personal Health Plan*. Share with your partner how your time with God went this week. What is one thing you discovered? Or, what obstacles hindered you from following through? Make a note about your partner's progress and how you can pray for him or her.

2. What do you think heaven looks like?

Growing

In chapter 4 John is given a special gift—he is taken to the "throne room" in heaven. He describes the magnificence of what he sees. He is also shown a sealed scroll. Who is worthy to open the seals? The answer is revealed in chapter 4.
   Read Revelation 4.

3. Where is John in 4:1 and where is he taken (v. 2)?

   Who is sitting on the throne? What do you think John means when he says this person has "the appearance of jasper and ruby" (v. 3)?

4. Read the *Study Notes* to understand the symbolism of the beings and objects in the throne room (4:3–11). Which aspects of the symbolism stand out to you as especially vivid or significant?
   ☐ Throne with the one seated on it
   ☐ Twenty-four thrones for twenty-four elders around the main throne
   ☐ Seven lamps of fire
   ☐ Four living creatures (cherubim)

5. What do you think this picture of the throne room is meant to reveal about God?

6. What do verses 8 and 11 tell us about how God should be approached?

   What is noteworthy to you about the things these beings say about God in these two verses?

Read Revelation 5.

7. In 5:1–5, John sees a sealed book (scroll). Only one person is worthy to open the seals of this unnamed legal document. Why is he worthy and no one else (see also vv. 9–10)?

8. John describes a scene with "the Lamb" in verses 6–14. Who is the Lamb? What is special about the Lamb?

9. Read Revelation 7:9–17. What do these verses tell us about God? About the Lamb?

10. John was Jewish, raised to see his people as set apart from all other ethnic groups as God's chosen "kingdom of priests" (Exod. 19:6). What do you make of the fact that he twice mentions "members of every tribe and language and people and nation" (5:9; compare 7:9)?

11. Of what value to us today is this glimpse into the throne room of heaven?

Only one person is worthy to open the sealed scroll and reveal God's future—Jesus Christ. He earned that honor by suffering and dying for our sins. God made sure that Jesus received his reward for faithfulness.

 Developing

God has blessed each of us with a unique set of gifts. He also calls for us to use those gifts to help others. One of John's gifts was the gift of evangelism—spreading the Gospel and message of Jesus Christ to unbelievers.

12. Brainstorm some ways you as a group can meet someone's physical needs. Consider collecting items for a local crisis pregnancy center. Maybe you know of an elderly person who could use help with some household chores or yard work. You best know the needs of your neighbors and community. Commit to picking a project and a date by next week.

13. The Bible reveals the many spiritual gifts given to believers. Take five minutes and review the *Spiritual Gifts Inventory* in the *Appendix*. Discuss which of the listed gifts you believe you may have.

    Once you have an idea about what your spiritual gifts are, discuss how your specific gift(s) might meet a need within your small group. For example, the gift of administration might meet the need to keep the roster updated; or the gift of hospitality might be used to plan a group social activity.

Sharing

"And do not forget to do good and to share with others, for with such sacrifices God is pleased" (Heb. 13:16 NIV). God's instructions are clear: we must share his good news with others.

14. If you are having trouble following through on your commitment to share with the people in your *Circles of Life*, pray right now for God's enabling power. Then, make a commitment to take the next step this week. Enlist your spiritual partner to pray for you and hold you accountable to your goals.

15. Telling your own story is a powerful way to share Jesus with others. Turn to *Telling Your Story* in the *Appendix*. Review this with your spiritual partner. Begin developing your story by taking a few minutes to share briefly what your life was like before you knew Christ. (If you haven't yet committed

your life to Christ or are not sure, you can find information about this in the *Sharing* section of *Session Three*. If you became a Christian at a very young age and don't remember what life was like before Christ, reflect on what you have seen in the life of someone close to you.) Make notes about this aspect of your story below and commit to writing it out this week. Then, spend some time individually developing your complete story using the *Telling Your Story* exercise in the Appendix.

_____

_____

_____

 Surrendering

In today's lesson we learned about the attendants in the throne room of heaven. These attendants spend all of their time worshiping and praising God. They are completely dedicated to the Lord, and an example of where we should place our devotion.

16. Share your praises and prayer requests with one another. Record these on the *Prayer and Praise Report*.

Study Notes

Throne: A rainbow resembling an emerald encircles the throne. God is radiant, and he is surrounded by brilliance, a symbol of sovereign rule and authority.

Twenty-four Elders: These may represent the twelve tribes of Israel (Old Testament) and the twelve apostles (New Testament), signifying the redeemed in joint rule with Christ. They are dressed in white (purity) and wear golden crowns (royalty). Twenty-four is the number associated with the priestly service and may be symbolic of the church operating in her role as priest.

Seven Lamps of Fire: Blazing lamps, representing the sevenfold Spirit of God—the Holy Spirit. Seven is the number of completeness identifying the fullness of the Holy Spirit.

Four Living Creatures (Cherubim): The prophet Ezekiel saw four living creatures, each with four faces: human in front, lion on the right, ox on the left, and eagle behind (Ezek. 1:6–10). John sees similar creatures: a lion, an ox, a flying eagle, and one with the face of a man. They reflect the presence, power, and holiness of God. These creatures give glory, honor and thanks to God.

Seven Seals: This indicates absolute sacredness; thus, only Jesus could open them.

For Deeper Study (Optional)

Read Ezekiel chapter 1. Note the similarities between Ezekiel's vision of heaven and John's (as we have studied thus far). Also note the differences between the two descriptions.

Reflections

Second Timothy 3:16–17 reads: "All Scripture is God-breathed and is useful for teaching, rebuking, correcting and training in righteousness, so that the man of God may be thoroughly equipped for every good work" (NIV). Allow God's Word to train you in righteousness as you read, reflect on, and respond to the Scripture in your daily time with God this week.

Day 1. See, the Lion of the tribe of Judah, the Root of David, has triumphed. He is able to open the scroll and its seven seals (Rev. 5:5 NIV).

REFLECT

_____
_____
_____
_____

Day 2. You are worthy to take the scroll and to open its seals, because you were slain, and with your blood you purchased men for God from every tribe and language and people and nation (Rev. 5:9 NIV).

REFLECT

_____
_____
_____
_____

Day 3. Worthy is the Lamb, who was slain, to receive power and wealth and wisdom and strength and honor and glory and praise! (Rev. 5:12 NIV).

REFLECT

_____
_____
_____
_____

Day 4. To him who sits on the throne and to the Lamb be praise and honor and glory and power, for ever and ever (Rev. 5:13 NIV).

REFLECT

_____
_____

_____

_____

Day 5. Salvation belongs to our God, who sits on the throne, and to the Lamb (Rev. 7:10 NIV).

REFLECT

_____

_____

_____

_____

Day 6. Use the following space to record your summary of how God has challenged you this week.

SUMMARY

_____

_____

_____

_____

JUDGMENT

Memory Verse: How long, O Lord, holy and true, will You refrain from judging and avenging our blood on those who dwell on the earth? (Rev. 6:10 NASB).

The FBI has maintained a Ten Most Wanted List since 1950. These are criminals who are deemed "dangerous" by the FBI. Some of them are on the run for years, even decades. They change their names, their appearance, even their nationality by moving to a foreign country. They go to great extremes to evade capture. But eventually most of them are caught. They are arrested, tried, convicted, and finally punished for their crimes. Despite efforts to avoid it, they can't escape judgment.

According to God, those who sin and are unrepentant will also receive judgment. God has promised judgment is coming. Revelation explains the reasons why judgment is necessary, and how punishment will be meted out.

Connecting

Open your group with prayer and invite the Holy Spirit to guide you as you participate in this session.

1. Check in with your spiritual partner, or with another partner if yours is absent. Talk about any challenges you are currently facing in reaching the goals you have set throughout this study. Tell your spiritual partner how he or she has encouraged you with each step. Be sure to write down your partner's progress.

2. Sharing a meal is a great way to get to know the others in your group better. During *Session Three*, you should have discussed whether your group would like to have a potluck or social. Take a few minutes now to tie up any loose ends in your plan.

3. Imagine that one of your co-workers unfairly receives a promotion—a promotion you wanted and believed you earned. How do you handle your disappointment?

 ## Growing

God's righteousness will not be denied. Throughout the Scriptures he promises that the wicked will receive their judgment. In this session we discover in detail how his justice will be expressed. In chapter 5, Christ was the only one found worthy to open the scroll—the title deed to the world. As he breaks the seven seals that secure the scroll, each seal unleashes a new demonstration of God's judgment on the earth in the future Tribulation period. The seventh seal then leads to the seven trumpets, and the seventh trumpet leads to the seven bowls.

Judgment	Verse	Symbolism
Seal One	6:1–2	Conquest (perhaps the reign of the Antichrist)
Seal Two	6:3–4	Human conflict on earth
Seal Three	6:5–6	Famine on earth
Seal Four	6:7–8	Death on earth
Seal Five	6:9–11	Persecution on earth
Seal Six	6:12–17	Mega-natural disasters
Seal Seven	8:1–5	Silence in heaven for a short time. The seven trumpets and seven bowls.
Trumpet One	8:7	Ravaging fires

Judgment	Verse	Symbolism
Trumpet Two	8:8–9	Seas polluted
Trumpet Three	8:10–11	Fresh water contaminated
Trumpet Four	8:12–13	Celestial disruption
Trumpet Five	9:1–12	Demonic invasion
Trumpet Six	9:13–21	Demons wage war
Trumpet Seven	11:15–19	Opening of the temple
Bowl One	16:2	Incurable skin sores
Bowl Two	16:3	Death of all sea creatures
Bowl Three	16:4–7	Freshwater turns to blood
Bowl Four	16:8–9	Humans scorched with great heat
Bowl Five	16:10–11	Worldwide darkness
Bowl Six	16:12–16	Armageddon
Bowl Seven	16:17–21	The Day of the Lord

Read Revelation 6:1–8:5, the Seal Judgments.

4. How does 6:9–11 explain why God must judge humanity so drastically? (See also 16:5–7 and 19:2.)

5. The seal judgments in 6:1–8:5 avenge the murders of the souls in 6:9–11. Why were these souls murdered?

What do the seal judgments suggest about God's view of evil?

6. In 8:1–5, what do you think the "silence in heaven" represents?

Read Revelation 8:6–11:19, the Trumpet Judgments.

7. The seal judgments are followed by the trumpet judgments. A fraction (one third) is used to approximate how much destruction there is in the earth, sea, rivers, and the moon and stars. Why do you think God chose one third? What might this amount suggest?

8. What are the scorpion-like locusts instructed to do in verses 9:3–6? What are they told not to do?

9. In 9:20–21, John writes how the people not killed by the plagues are still sinning and refusing to repent. What might be possible reasons or causes of their stubbornness?

Read 15:5–16:21, the Bowl Judgments.

10. The seven bowls represent the wrath of God. What happens after the bowls are emptied on the earth?

11. Look at 11:16–19. How do the twenty-four elders respond to all the terrifying things that have happened?

   How do these verses reveal God's righteousness?

12. Despite the horrific consequences of sin expressed by God's judgments, John says there will be a remnant of people who will be victorious in the end. Read the passages listed below. Who are the remnant in each passage?
   ☐ Revelation 6:9–11
   ☐ Revelation 7:4–8
   ☐ Revelation 7:9–17
   ☐ Revelation 11:3–12

13. What do you think is the purpose of the judgments?

14. What do you take away from this portion of Revelation? What thoughts about God, for example? About yourself? About life?

This portion of Scripture can seem frightening. The judgments are harsh but necessary because of the behavior of the unrepentant. Yet even in his judgment, God offers hope to those who persevere. They will come through the tribulation *victorious*.

Developing

According to the book of Acts, the early Christian church made it a priority to serve each other. They ate together, cared for the widows and the poor, and pooled their resources. Serving with and for others is an excellent way to strengthen your faith and your spirit.

15. This week, discuss how you may be able to use your gifts to serve beyond this small group to the ministries in your church and plan to get involved in serving the body of Christ right away. It's amazing to experience God using you to fill a specific need within his church.

16. On your *Personal Health Plan*, in the "Develop" section, answer the "WHERE are you serving?" question. If you are not currently serving, note one area where you will consider serving and commit to praying for the right opportunity and time to begin.

Sharing

Jesus could have kept his revelation a secret, but instead he shared it with the world through the apostle John. We should follow Christ's example and share God's plan for our lives with unbelievers.

17. In *Session Two*, you identified people within your *Circles of Life* that needed connection to Christian community. Jesus's commission in Acts 1:8 says: "But you will receive power when the Holy Spirit comes on you; and you will be my witnesses in Jerusalem, and in all Judea and Samaria, and to the ends of the earth" (NIV). Jesus intended for his followers to share him not only within our own circles of influence (our Jerusalem), but also in Judea and Samaria and the ends of the earth. Judea included the region in which Jerusalem was located. Today, this includes our neighboring communities or cities. As a group, discuss the following possible actions you can take to share Jesus with your Judea in a tangible way.

- ☐ Collect children's books or school supplies to donate to needy schools in a nearby community.

- ☐ Donate basic personal care items to a local convalescent home or assisted care facility for the elderly. Plan to deliver the items together and spend an hour or two visiting with lonely residents.

- ☐ Contact your local mission or homeless shelter and ask how your group might be able to volunteer. Some offer opportunities to donate handwritten holiday or birthday cards that they give to their residents.

Surrendering

When writing his letters, Paul never forgot to thank Christians for their prayers. "We were under great pressure, far beyond our ability to endure," he writes in 2 Corinthians 1:8. He continues in verses 10 and 11: "On him we have set our hope that he will continue to deliver us, as you help us by your prayers" (NIV). Paul understood the priceless power of prayer.

18. Have someone volunteer to read Psalm 23 out loud while the rest of the group considers it in light of what it means to be sheep under the care of the Good Shepherd.

19. Don't forget to share your praises and prayer requests with one another and conclude your group time in prayer.

Study Notes

The Four Horses: this imagery has its basis in Zechariah 1:8–17, and 6:1–8. White symbolizes conquest, red symbolizes bloodshed and war, black symbolizes famine, and gray or ashen symbolizes death.

Seven Trumpets: During Old Testament times, the trumpet announced important events and gave signals of war.

For Deeper Study (Optional)

To further understand the judgments, fill in the following chart concerning the seal, bowl, and trumpet judgments. The first judgment is completed as an example for you to follow.

Judgment No.	The Seal Judgments	The Trumpet Judgments	The Bowl Judgments
1	White horse, sent out to conquer (6:1–2)	Hail and fire mixed with blood, ⅓ of earth scorched (8:7)	Loathsome malignant sore on people (16:2)
2			
3			
4			
5			
6			
7			

Reflections

The Lord promised Joshua success and prosperity in Joshua 1:8 when he said: "Do not let this Book of the Law depart from your mouth; meditate on it day and night, so that you may be careful to do everything written in it. Then you will be prosperous and successful" (NIV). We too can claim this promise for our lives as we commit to meditate on the Word of God each day. As in previous weeks, read and meditate on the daily verses and record any prayers or insights you gain in the space provided. Summarize what you have learned this week on Day Six.

Day 1. They are before the throne of God and serve him day and night in his temple, and he who sits on the throne will spread his tent over them (Rev. 7:15 NIV).

REFLECT

_____

_____

_____

_____

Day 2. Never again will they hunger; never again will they thirst. The sun will not beat upon them, not any scorching heat (Rev. 7:16 NIV).

REFLECT

_____

_____

_____

_____

Day 3. For the Lamb at the center of the throne will be their shepherd; he will lead them to springs of living water. And God will wipe away every tear from their eyes (Rev. 7:17 NIV).

REFLECT

_____

_____

_____

_____

Day 4. You are just in these judgments, you who are and who were, the Holy One, because you have so judged (Rev. 16:5 NIV).

REFLECT

_____

_____

_____

_____

Day 5. For they have shed the blood of your saints and prophets, and you have given them blood to drink as they deserve (Rev. 16:6 NIV).

REFLECT

_____

_____

_____

_____

Day 6. Use the following space to write any thoughts God has put in your heart and mind during *Session Five* and your *Reflections* time this week.

SUMMARY

_____

_____

_____

_____

PERSECUTION

Memory Verse: To him who overcomes, I will give the right to sit with me on my throne, just as I overcame and sat down with my Father on his throne (Rev. 3:21 NIV).

After becoming a widow in 1905, Elizabeth, the Grand Duchess of Russia, sold and gave away all her possessions, including her wedding ring, and founded the Convents of Saints Martha and Mary. She became its abbess, and opened a hospital, a pharmacy, and an orphanage, as well. She worked relentlessly in the slums of Moscow, determined to do what she could to alleviate the suffering of the poor. In 1918 she was martyred by the Bolsheviks, along with several of her relatives, being clubbed on the head and thrown into a pit. It is said that while the victims were in the pit, the murderers could hear Elizabeth and the others singing a Russian hymn. Her remains were taken to Jerusalem, where they lie today in the Church of Maria Magdalene.

Elizabeth's story is only one of many throughout history. From the first Christian martyr, Stephen, to those killed for their faith in contemporary times, the persecution of Christians continues. According to Revelation, there will be a time of even greater persecution during the final days. But as always, God gives peace to sufferers and strength to the oppressed.

Connecting

Open your group with prayer and invite the Holy Spirit to guide you through your study time.

1. Check in with your spiritual partner, or with another partner if yours is absent. Share your progress and any challenges you are currently facing. Take a few minutes to pray for each other now.

2. How do you typically respond when you see someone treated unfairly?

Growing

John wrote Revelation to Christians facing discrimination and even arrest and death for their faith. He called himself their "brother and companion in the suffering and kingdom and patient endurance that are ours in Jesus" (1:9 NIV). He wanted them to understand that Christians should expect to suffer and should plan on developing patient endurance. His visions consistently offer encouragement to those who remain faithful under pressure.

3. In chapters 2–3, the churches have several temptations to overcome: Social pressure tempts them to compromise God's moral standards and alter the gospel. They are also tempted to renounce Christ under threat of death. Jesus promises rewards to those who overcome these pressures. Which of the following rewards are motivating to you, and why?

   ☐ The crown of (eternal) life for those who are willing to die for their faith (2:10)

   ☐ A white stone with God's hidden name on it, your engraved invitation to God's heavenly banquet (2:17)

- ☐ Authority to rule over the nations (2:26–27)
- ☐ The morning star (2:28)—Jesus himself (see 22:16)
- ☐ White robes (of purity), your name in the book of life, and Jesus acknowledging you before the Father and his angels (3:5)
- ☐ The name of Christ, and the Father, and their city inscribed on you (3:12)
- ☐ The right to sit with Jesus on his throne (3:21)

4. God's intense judgment is referred to as the Great Tribulation. John sees a number of episodes in this Tribulation. One episode, in 11:1–14, involves two witnesses. Describe the task God gives to these two witnesses (vv. 3–6).

What price do these witnesses pay for doing what God has asked of them (vv. 7–10)?

Describe their reward (vv. 11–12).

What would it take for you to speak for God in a corrupt generation if you knew that humiliation and death would be the consequence?

5. John also sees war in heaven: God's angels versus Satan and his angels (12:7–9). Read the proclamation from heaven after Satan is cast out (12:10–12). Why do you think Satan is called "the accuser of our brothers"?

Explain in your own words how the brothers (believers) triumph over Satan (v. 11).

Is this helpful information for you? If so, how?

6. Read chapter 13, which describes what God's people have to endure in the Tribulation. What are some of the ways they suffer?

What does it take to remain faithful to God under such pressure?

7. Why do we need to know all this about suffering and reward?

8. Has there been a time in your life when you faced persecution or pressure to compromise your faith? If so, how did you respond?

   How will God's promises help you the next time you experience pressure to act against your faith?

God is righteous and just. He will not tolerate sin, and he shows grace to those who are steadfastly his. The Lord's redemptive plan is not merely one of brimstone and fire, but of mercy and love. Yet during the period when God allows evil forces to do their worst, he asks his people to remain faithful and boldly stand for goodness and truth.

 ### Developing

Self-pity seems to come easily when we are going through difficult times in our lives. Yet one of the best ways to forget about our own troubles is to focus on someone else. Helping others not only gets our mind off of whatever bothers us, it also makes us feel good. We might even realize that our problems aren't as bad as we thought they were.

9. To serve as Jesus did, we need to be willing to humble ourselves to carry out even the most menial of tasks. This could mean doing yard work, painting a house, or cleaning for someone who is in need. If time permits during this session, discuss with one another how you might serve a needy family in your church. Devise a game plan and then commit to seeing it through. You could choose one or two people who are willing to follow up with your church or a local ministry to put your plan into action.

10. If you've been spending time with God each day, consider journaling as a way to grow even closer to God. Read through *Journaling 101* found in the *Appendix*. Commit this week to spending a portion of your time with God writing your thoughts and prayers in a journal.

11. Briefly discuss the future of your group. How many of you are willing to stay together as a group and work through another study together? If you have time, turn to the *Small Group Agreement* and talk about any changes you would like to make as you move forward as a group.

Sharing

"Command them to do good, to be rich in good deeds, and to be generous and willing to share" (1 Tim. 6:18 NIV). This was Paul's charge to Timothy and the church at Ephesus. These instructions are just as important today as they were when Paul wrote them.

12. Return to the *Circles of Life* diagram now. Outside each circle, write down one or two names of people you know who need to know Christ. Commit to praying for an opportunity to share Jesus with each of them. You may invite them to attend an outreach event with you or you may feel led to share the good news with him or her over coffee. Share your commitment with your spiritual partner. Pray together for God's Holy Spirit to give you the words to speak with boldness.

13. Telling your own story is a powerful way to share Jesus with others. Yet many people are challenged in sharing Jesus with others because they feel they don't know what to say. You don't have to have a polished, complicated testimony to share your story. You simply tell what Jesus has done for you. Turn to *Telling Your Story* in the *Appendix*. Review this with your spiritual partner. Begin developing your story by taking a few minutes to share briefly what your life was like before you knew Christ. (If you haven't yet committed your life to Christ or are

not sure, you can find information about this in the *Sharing* section of *Session Three*. If you became a Christian at a very young age and don't remember what life was like before Christ, reflect on what you have seen in the life of someone close to you.) Make notes about this aspect of your story below and commit to writing it out this week. Then, spend some time individually developing your complete story using the *Telling Your Story* exercise in the *Appendix*.

14. On your *Personal Health Plan*, in the "Sharing" section, answer the "WHEN are you shepherding another person in Christ?" question.

 Surrendering

What pleases God? Our devotion to him, our kindness to others, our excitement about our faith—these are only a few things that make us pleasing in his sight.

15. Share your praises and prayer requests with one another. Record these on the *Prayer and Praise Report*. Then end your time by praying for each other.

Study Notes

The Beast: The beast is the major opponent of Christians in the final days. Since he comes up from the abyss, he is of demonic nature.

Their Bodies Will Lie in the Streets (11:8): In ancient times the lack of a proper burial was extremely humiliating.

White Robes: Represent holiness and purity.

For Deeper Study (Optional)

Read the verses below and identify what each one says about the persecution of the church and the faith of the believers.

Revelation 14:1–5
Revelation 20:4–6
Revelation 21:3–4

Reflections

Get into harmony with God as you spend time with him this week. Read and reflect on the daily verses. Then record your thoughts, insights, or prayers in the *Reflect* sections that follow. On the sixth day record your summary of what God has taught you this week.

Day 1. Great and marvelous are your deeds, Lord God Almighty. Just and true are your ways, King of the ages (Rev. 15:3 NIV).

REFLECT

_____

_____

_____

_____

Day 2. Who will not fear you, O Lord, and bring glory to your name? For you alone are holy. All nations will come and worship before you, for your righteous acts have been revealed (Rev. 15:4 NIV).

REFLECT

_____

_____

_____

_____

Day 3. Yes, Lord God Almighty, true and just are your judgments (Rev. 16:7 NIV).

REFLECT

_____

_____

_____

_____

Day 4. If anyone is to go into captivity, into captivity he will go. If anyone is to be killed with the sword, with the sword he will be killed. This calls for patient endurance and faithfulness on the part of the saints (Rev. 13:10 NIV).

REFLECT

_____

_____

_____

_____

Day 5. Then I saw another angel flying in midair, and he had the eternal gospel to proclaim to those who live on the earth—to every nation, tribe, language and people. He said in a loud voice, "Fear God, and give him glory, because the hour of his judgment has come. Worship him who made the heavens, the earth, the sea and the springs of water" (Rev. 14:6–7 NIV).

REFLECT

_____

_____

_____

_____

Day 6. Record your summary of what God has taught you this week.

SUMMARY

_____

_____

_____

_____

THE PROSTITUTE

Memory Verse: Woe! Woe, O great city, O Babylon, city of power! In one hour your doom has come! (Rev. 18:10 NIV).

In the 1990s, Enron, an American energy company based in Texas, was considered one of the top companies in the United States. In 2000, its revenues topped over 100 billion dollars. However, it was revealed during the following year that Enron's executives had staged one of the most complex and corrupt episodes of corporate fraud ever uncovered. The company filed bankruptcy, resulting in the lay-offs of thousands of employees. Not only had these workers lost their jobs, but their pensions were wiped out. For a great number of them, their pensions represented their total life savings. Amidst the tragedy of its workforce, Enron executives still maintained many of their assets. As people scrambled to find new jobs and figure out a way to salvage their future, those who had perpetrated the fraud failed to make restitution. The people in charge of Enron had fallen prey to greed and power, with disastrous results.

In Revelation, Babylon the prostitute represents the evil world system to which the Enron executives succumbed. But God's people are called to live in preparation for the New Jerusalem rather than to be molded by the immorality and rebellion of the evil world system.

 ## Connecting

Open your group with prayer and invite the Holy Spirit to guide you as you participate in this session.

1. Check in with your spiritual partner, or with another partner if yours is absent. Share your progress and any challenges you are currently facing. Consider checking in by e-mail or phone throughout the week if you both would like to. Take a few minutes to pray for each other now. Be sure to write down your partner's progress.

2. Share at least one way God has worked in your life since you began this study.

 ## Growing

Revelation 17–18 is filled with intense imagery regarding a woman and a beast. An angel is on hand to explain these things to John, who faithfully records them.
    Read chapter 17.

3. The great harlot or prostitute is symbolically named "Babylon," the Old Testament empire that destroyed Jerusalem and took God's people into exile. In Revelation, "Babylon" probably represents the Roman Empire, which was actively persecuting God's people in John's day. In a larger sense what do you think the prostitute Babylon represents today?

    What are the prostitute's sins (17:2, 6)? Do you think John is talking mainly about literal, physical adultery, or are there other ways people commit "adultery" with "Babylon"?

4. The woman is riding a beast (17:3). The symbolism in 17:8–18 would have been clearer to John's readers than to us: The woman is imperial Rome (whose seven hills, 17:9, were famous). The beast is a ruler, antichrist. The main point of this section is a war between two opposing powers. According to 17:12–16, who are the two sides in this war?

What is the outcome of the war, and why?

Why does this matter to us?

5. According to 17:17, the beast has all this power to do evil solely because God has temporarily given it that power. What do you make of this? Why do you suppose God lets the beast have power?

Read chapter 18.

6. In verses 1–8, how is the prostitute ultimately destroyed?

Who lament over her death, and why (18:9–20)?

When you think about the world system that is so powerful even now, before the end, how does chapter 18 move you to regard that system?

7. What do chapters 17–18 tell you about where we should place our faith?

Where is your faith based—in the world, or in God? What is the evidence?

The world we live in is filled with evil and corruption. God's people are called to resist the wickedness of this world. Although the battle isn't easy, God, in his great and mighty power, will overcome the world and the beast. He will prepare for his faithful a new place, a New Jerusalem.

Developing

While helping others can be a rewarding experience, there may be times when giving of our time and talents might seem like a burden, especially if our own schedule is overloaded. During those times it is important to ask God for the strength and energy to be in his will.

8. First Corinthians 12:7 says: "A spiritual gift is given to each of us as a means of helping the entire church" (NLT). Review the *Spiritual Gifts Inventory* in the *Appendix* once again. As you read through the different gifts, make a star or checkmark next to those that you think you have. If you haven't already done so, share what you believe your spiritual gifts are. If you have discovered a ministry in which to serve, share where you found the opportunities to exercise your gift(s), either within the small group, or in your church. This could serve as encouragement to those who are struggling to find a ministry.

   If you know your gifts but have not yet plugged into a ministry, discuss how your gifts might meet a need within your church. Make a commitment to take the necessary steps to get plugged into that ministry. Or if your group is continuing beyond this study of Revelation, choose an area to begin serving within the small group.

   If you still do not know what your spiritual gift(s) are, review the inventory with a trusted friend who knows you well. Chances are they have witnessed one or more of these gifts in your life.

Sharing

"So do not fear, for I am with you" (Isa. 41:10 NIV). Speaking out about your faith can be an uncomfortable experience, especially if you are not sure how you will be received by unbelievers. As we learned in today's session, the world is filled with people who persecute and reject Christians.

9. Several of you share how acts of selflessness have touched your lives or how you have used those acts to reach others.

10. During *Session Four* you discussed ways you as a group can meet someone's physical needs. If you brought items to donate tonight, spend a few minutes praying for the individuals or families that will receive them. If you have planned to serve in another way, finalize those plans now. Don't pass up the opportunity to serve the body of Christ in this tangible way.

 Surrendering

Jesus fully surrendered to the Father's will, even to the point of a terrible death. Most of us won't be asked to sacrifice nearly to that extent, but he does want our hearts completely.

11. Turn to the *Personal Health Plan* and individually consider the "HOW are you surrendering your heart?" question. Look to the *Sample Personal Health Plan* for help. Share some of your thoughts in the group.

12. Share your prayer requests and record them on the *Prayer and Praise Report*. Have any previous prayer requests been answered? If so, celebrate these answers to prayer. Then, in simple, one-sentence prayers, submit your requests to God and close by thanking God for his commitment to your relationship with him and how he has used this group to teach you more about faith.

Study Notes

Abyss: Means "very deep" or "bottomless" in Greek.

Armageddon: Probably stands for Har Mageddon, "the mountain of Megiddo." Megiddo was a city in lower Galilee (Judg. 5:19), but there is no obvious mountain associated with it. The name may refer to the plain of Megiddo (2 Chron. 35:22; Zech. 12:11) or may serve as a symbolic name for the place of God's final conquering of evil.

Mystery: A secret reserved in heaven and revealed to the apocalyptist (John).

For Deeper Study (Optional)

Today's study discussed the fall of Babylon. Read Revelation chapter 18 and see if you can identify the elements of description, prophecies, and destruction of Babylon.

Description of Babylon   She has become a home for demons and a haunt for every evil spirit (Rev. 18:2)

Prophecies about Babylon

Destruction of Babylon

Reflections

As you read the given verse each day, prayerfully consider what you learn about God, his Spirit, and his place in your life. Then record your thoughts, insights, or prayer in the *Reflect* section below the verses you read. On the sixth day record a summary of what you have learned over the entire week through this study.

Day 1. With her the kings of the earth committed adultery and the inhabitants of the earth were intoxicated with the wine of her adulteries (Rev. 17:2 NIV).

REFLECT

_____

_____

73

_____

_____

Day 2. Her sins are piled up to heaven and God has remembered her crimes. Give back to her as she has given; pay her back double for what she has done. Mix her a double portion from her own cup (Rev. 18:5–6 NIV).

REFLECT

_____

_____

_____

_____

Day 3. Therefore in one day her plagues will overtake her; death, mourning and famine. She will be consumed by fire for mighty is the Lord God who judges her (Rev. 18:8 NIV).

REFLECT

_____

_____

_____

_____

Day 4. Then I saw a new heaven and a new earth, for the first heaven and the first earth had passed away, and there was no longer any sea. I saw the Holy City, the new Jerusalem, coming down out of heaven from God, prepared as a bride beautifully dressed for her husband (Rev. 21:1–2 NIV).

REFLECT

_____

_____

_____

_____

Day 5. He will wipe away every tear from their eyes. There will be no more death or mourning or crying or pain, for the old order of things has passed away (Rev. 21:4 NIV).

REFLECT

_____

_____

_____

_____

Day 6. Use the following space to summarize what God has revealed to you during *Session Seven* and the *Reflections*.

SUMMARY

_____

_____

_____

_____

HOPE

Memory Verse: He who was seated on the throne said, "I am making everything new!" Then he said, "Write this down, for these words are trustworthy and true" (Rev. 21:5 NIV).

Marathon runners maintain a grueling training schedule. It is not unusual for them to run between thirty and forty miles a week when preparing for a big race. They must take into account their nutritional needs, often denying themselves delicious sweets and treats in lieu of food that gives them the maximum amount of energy. The constant pounding of their feet on asphalt and concrete takes its toll on their bodies, and many runners are constantly battling muscle pain and injuries. To be an accomplished marathoner requires dedication, sacrifice, and perseverance.

During the end times, Christians will be in a marathon of their own, and the stakes are higher than we can imagine. Believers must derive their spiritual strength and energy from the Lord to survive the lengthy trials and persecution ahead. But for the Christian who perseveres, the reward of a lifetime awaits.

Connecting

Open your group with prayer and come together one last time for this session as we study the Lord's death and resurrection.

During this eight-session study we hope you have discovered the importance of connecting with other Christians through fellowship and support. Be sure to continue reaching out and supporting others after this study is over.

1. Take time in this final session to connect with your spiritual partner. What has God been showing you through these sessions about the life of Jesus? Check in with each other about the progress you have made in your spiritual growth during this study. Make plans about whether you will continue in your mentoring relationship outside your Bible study group.

2. Share one thing that you have discovered about God or something that has challenged or encouraged you during this study.

Growing

After the time of tribulation, the devil is defeated and Christians emerge victorious. God has a special place for his faithful. The final chapters of Revelation reveal the wonderful reward in store.

Read Revelation 21.

3. Compare Revelation 21:1 to Genesis 1:1. How has the Bible come full circle?

Instead of the prostitute city, Babylon, we have the holy city adorned as a bride, the new Jerusalem (Rev. 21:2). What is personally significant to you in 21:3–4?

Why is that significant to you?

4. What impression do you get of the holy city from 21:9–21?

   What aspects of 21:22–27 are especially appealing to you, and why?

5. While some of us might imagine paradise as solitude in a beautiful wilderness, our true destiny is a beautiful city, a place where there will be lots of other people, as well as God. How do you respond to the idea that your destiny is a city?

Read Revelation 22.

6. Within the city, John sees a river and a tree, the restoration of the garden of Eden inside the city. What do you think we can learn about this place from details like the water of life, and the tree of life with its healing leaves (22:1–2)?

7. Why do you think the statement, "Look, I am coming soon!" is repeated twice (22:7, 12 NLT)?

8. In 22:17, what do you think it means to be "thirsty"?

   How does a person come and take this gift?

9. What practical, daily difference do you think God wants this glimpse of your destiny to make to the way you live now?

The culmination of God's redemptive plan is the opportunity to live with him and each other for eternity, with abundant life and no sorrow. Christians who are suffering can find strength in this promise. God has been and will always be just and generous.

Developing

Whether you continue with this group or not, continue to seek ways to help fellow Christians, and prayerfully seek wisdom to develop your unique talents to further God's kingdom.

10. If your group still needs to make decisions about continuing to meet after this session, have that discussion now. Talk about what you will study, who will lead, and where and when you will meet.

Review your *Small Group Agreement* and evaluate how well you met your goals. Discuss any changes you want to make as you move forward. As your group starts a new study this is a great time to take on a new role or change roles of service in your group. What new role will you take on? If you are uncertain, maybe your group members have some ideas for you. Remember you aren't making a lifetime commitment to the new role; it will only be for a few weeks. Maybe someone would like to share a role with you if you don't feel ready to serve solo.

Sharing

The hope we have in God's wonderful plan of redemption is too good to keep for ourselves! Commit to continue sharing your knowledge and enthusiasm with others in your community through the outreach activities your group developed in this study.

11. During the course of this study, you have made commitments to share Jesus with the people in your life, either by inviting your friends to grow in Christian community or by sharing the Gospel in words or actions with unbelievers. Share with the group any highlights that you experienced as you stepped out in faith to share with others.

Surrendering

Surrender to the Lord is not a one time occurrence, it is a lifetime commitment. One way to grow closer to God is to worship him together in a meaningful way.

12. Close by praying for your prayer requests and take a couple of minutes to review the praises you have recorded over the past few weeks on the *Prayer and Praise Report*. Thank God for what he's done in your group during this study.

Study Notes

Dwelling Place, Dwell (21:3): The noun is the word for the Old Testament tabernacle; the related verb is used in John 1:14.

Bride: The church, the people of God, is called the bride of Christ (2 Cor. 11:2; Eph. 5:23).

The Holy City: It merges characteristics of the garden of Eden, Jerusalem, and the temple in Jerusalem. The city's shape, a perfect cube (Rev. 21:16), is the shape of the Holy of Holies in the temple. The numbers used to describe it are 12 (the number of the tribes and apostles) and multiples of 12 and 10 (the walls are 144 cubits thick, the city is a cube of 12,000 × 12,000 × 12,000 stadia). The numbers 12, 10, and 7 are symbolic throughout Revelation.

The Tree of Life: See Genesis 2:8–14; 3:22–24.

Reflections

As you read through this final week of *Reflections*, prayerfully consider what God is showing you about his character, the Holy Spirit, and how he wants you to grow and change. Then, write down your thoughts or prayers in the space provided. Don't let this concluding week of *Reflections* be your last. Commit to continue reading, reflecting, and meditating on the Word of God daily. Use Day Six to record your prayer of commitment to see this discipline become habit.

Day 1. He who overcomes will inherit all this, and I will be his God and he will be my son (Rev. 21:7 NIV).

REFLECT

_____

_____

_____

_____

Day 2. But the cowardly, the unbelieving, the vile, the murderers, the sexually immoral, those who practice magic arts, the idolaters and all liars—their place will be in the fiery lake of burning sulfur. This is the second death (Rev. 21:8 NIV).

REFLECT

_____

_____

_____

_____

Day 3. Now the dwelling of God is with men, and he will live with them. They will be his people, and God himself will be with them and be their God (Rev. 21:3 NIV).

REFLECT

_____

_____

_____

_____

Day 4. Let him who does wrong continue to do wrong; let him who is vile continue to be vile; let him who does right continue to do right; and let him who is holy continue to be holy (Rev. 22:11 NIV).

REFLECT

_____

_____

_____

_____

Day 5. No longer will there be any curse. The throne of God and of the Lamb will be in the city, and his servants will serve him. They will see his face, and his name will be on their foreheads. There will be no more night. They will not need the light of a lamp or the light of the sun, for the Lord God will give them light. And they will reign for ever and ever (Rev. 22:3-5 NIV).

REFLECT

_____

_____

_____

_____

Day 6. Use the following space to write your prayer of commitment to continue spending time daily in God's Word and prayer.

SUMMARY

_____

_____

_____

_____

FREQUENTLY ASKED QUESTIONS

What do we do on the first night of our group?

Like all fun things in life—have a party! A "get to know you" coffee, dinner, or dessert is a great way to launch a new study. You may want to review the *Small Group Agreement* and share the names of a few friends you can invite to join you. But most importantly, have fun before your study time begins.

Where do we find new members for our group?

This can be challenging, especially for new groups that have only a few people or for existing groups that lose a few people along the way. We encourage you to pray with your group and then brainstorm a list of people from work, church, your neighborhood, your children's school, family, the gym, and so forth. Then have each group member invite several of the people on his or her list. Another good strategy is to ask church leaders to make an announcement that your group is open to new members.

No matter how you find members, it's vital that you stay on the lookout for new people to join your group. All groups tend to go through healthy attrition—the result of moves, releasing new leaders, ministry opportunities, and so forth—and if the group gets too small, it could be at risk of shutting down. If you and your group stay open, you'll be amazed at the people God sends your way. The next person just might become a friend for life. You never know!

How long will this group meet?

It's totally up to the group—once you come to the end of this study. Most groups meet weekly for at least their first six months together, but every other week can work as well. We strongly recommend that the group meet for the first six months on a weekly basis if at all possible. This allows for continuity, and if people miss a meeting they aren't gone for a whole month.

At the end of this study, each group member may decide whether he or she wants to continue on for another study. Some groups launch relationships that last for years, and others are stepping-stones into another group experience. Either way, enjoy the journey.

What if this group is not working for me?

Personality conflicts, life stage differences, geographical distance, level of spiritual maturity, or any number of things can cause you to feel the group doesn't work for you. Relax. Pray for God's direction, and at the end of this study decide whether to continue with this group or find another. You don't buy the first car you look at or marry the first person you date, and the same goes with a group. Don't bail out before the study is finished—God might have something to teach you. Also, don't run from conflict or prejudge people before you have given them a chance. God is still working in you too!

Who is the leader?

Most groups have an official leader. But ideally, the group will mature and members will share the facilitation of meetings. We have discovered that healthy groups share hosting and leading of the group. This model ensures that all members grow, give their unique contribution, and develop their gifts. This study guide and the Holy Spirit can keep things on track even when you share leadership. Christ has promised to be in your midst as you gather. Ultimately, God is your leader each step of the way.

How do we handle the child care needs in our group?

This can be a sensitive issue. We suggest that you empower the group to openly brainstorm solutions. You may try one option that works for a while and then adjust over time. Our favorite approach is for adults to meet in the living room or dining room, and share the cost of a babysitter (or two) who can be with the kids in a different part of the house. In this way, parents don't have to be away from their children all evening when their children are too young to be left at home. A second option is to use one home for the kids and a second home (close by) for the adults. A third idea is to rotate the responsibility of providing a lesson or care for the children either in the same home or in another home nearby. This can be an incredible blessing for kids. Finally, the most common idea is to decide that you need to have a night to invest in your spiritual lives individually or as a couple, and make your own arrangements for child care. No matter what decision the group makes, the best approach is to dialogue openly about both the problem and the solution.

SMALL GROUP AGREEMENT

Our Purpose

To transform our spiritual lives by cultivating our spiritual health in a healthy small group community. In addition, we:

_____

_____

_____

Our Values

Group Attendance	To give priority to the group meeting. We will call or e-mail if we will be late or absent. (Completing the *Small Group Calendar* will minimize this issue.)
Safe Environment	To help create a safe place where people can be heard and feel loved. (Please, no quick answers, snap judgments, or simple fixes.)
Respect Differences	To be gentle and gracious to people with different spiritual maturity, personal opinions, temperaments, or imperfections. We are all works in progress.
Confidentiality	To keep anything that is shared strictly confidential and within the group, and avoid sharing improper information about those outside the group.
Encouragement for Growth	To be not just takers but givers of life. We want to spiritually multiply our lives by serving others with our God-given gifts.

Welcome for Newcomers	To keep an open chair and share Jesus's dream of finding a shepherd for every sheep.
Shared Ownership	To remember that every member is a minister and to ensure that each attender will share a small team role or responsibility over time. (See the *Team Roles*.)
Rotating Hosts/ Leaders and Homes	To encourage different people to host the group in their homes, and to rotate the responsibility of facilitating each meeting. (See the *Small Group Calendar*.)

Our Expectations

- Refreshments/mealtimes _____
- Child care _____
- When we will meet (day of week) _____
- Where we will meet (place) _____
- We will begin at (time) _____ and end at _____
- We will do our best to have some or all of us attend a worship service together. Our primary worship service time will be _____
- Date of this agreement _____
- Date we will review this agreement again _____
- Who (other than the leader) will review this agreement at the end of this study _____

TEAM ROLES

The Bible makes clear that every member, not just the small group leader, is a minister in the body of Christ. In a healthy small group, every member takes on some small role or responsibility. It can be more fun and effective if you team up on these roles.

Review the team roles and responsibilities below, and have each member volunteer for a role or participate on a team. If someone doesn't know where to serve or is holding back, as a group, suggest a team or role. It's best to have one or two people on each team so you have each of the five purposes covered. Serving in even a small capacity will not only help your leader but also will make the group more fun for everyone. Don't hold back. Join a team!

The opportunities below are broken down by the five purposes and then by a *crawl* (beginning), *walk* (intermediate), or *run* (advanced) role. Try to cover at least the crawl and walk roles, and select a role that matches your group, your gifts, and your maturity.

Team Roles	Team Player(s)

CONNECTING TEAM (Fellowship and Community Building)

Crawl: Host a social event or group activity in the first week or two.

Walk: Create a list of uncommitted friends and then invite them to an open house or group social.

Run: Plan a twenty-four-hour retreat or weekend getaway for the group. Lead the *Connecting* time each week for the group.

GROWING TEAM (Discipleship and Spiritual Growth)

Crawl: Coordinate the spiritual partners for the group. Facilitate a three- or four-person discussion circle during the Bible study portion of your meeting. Coordinate the discussion circles.

Walk: Tabulate the *Personal Health Plans* in a summary to let people know how you're doing as a group. Encourage personal devotions through group discussions and pairing up with spiritual (accountability) partners.

Run: Take the group on a prayer walk, or plan a day of solitude, fasting, or personal retreat.

SERVING TEAM (Discovering Your God-Given Design for Ministry)

Crawl: Ensure that every member finds a group role or team he or she enjoys.

Walk: Have every member take a gift test and determine your group's gifts. Plan a ministry project together.

Run: Help each member decide on a way to use his or her unique gifts somewhere in the church.

SHARING TEAM (Sharing and Evangelism)

Crawl: Coordinate the group's *Prayer and Praise Report* of friends and family who don't know Christ.

Walk: Search for group mission opportunities and plan a cross-cultural group activity.

Run: Take a small group "vacation" to host a six-week group in your neighborhood or office. Then come back together with your current group.

SURRENDERING TEAM (Surrendering Your Heart to Worship)

Crawl: Maintain the group's *Prayer and Praise Report* or journal.

Walk: Lead a brief time of worship each week (at the beginning or end of your meeting).

Run: Plan a more unique time of worship.

89

SMALL GROUP CALENDAR

Planning and calendaring can help ensure the greatest participation at every meeting. At the end of each meeting, review this calendar. Be sure to include a regular rotation of host homes and leaders, and don't forget birthdays, socials, church events, holidays, and mission/ministry projects.

Date	Lesson	Dessert/Meal	Role

PERSONAL HEALTH ASSESSMENT

	Just Beginning	Getting Going	Well Developed

CONNECTING with God's Family

I am deepening my understanding of and friendship with God in community with others. — 1 2 3 4 5

I am growing in my ability both to share and to show my love to others. — 1 2 3 4 5

I am willing to share my real needs for prayer and support from others. — 1 2 3 4 5

I am resolving conflict constructively and am willing to forgive others. — 1 2 3 4 5

CONNECTING Total _____

GROWING to Be Like Christ

I have a growing relationship with God through regular time in the Bible and in prayer (spiritual habits). — 1 2 3 4 5

I am experiencing more of the characteristics of Jesus Christ (love, patience, gentleness, courage, self-control, etc.) in my life. — 1 2 3 4 5

I am avoiding addictive behaviors (food, television, busyness, and the like) to meet my needs. — 1 2 3 4 5

I am spending time with a Christian friend (spiritual partner) who celebrates and challenges my spiritual growth. — 1 2 3 4 5

GROWING Total _____

91

	Just Beginning	Getting Going	Well Developed

DEVELOPING Your Gifts to Serve Others

I have discovered and am further developing my unique God-given design.	1 2 3 4 5
I am regularly praying for God to show me opportunities to serve him and others.	1 2 3 4 5
I am serving in a regular (once a month or more) ministry in the church or community.	1 2 3 4 5
I am a team player in my small group by sharing some group role or responsibility.	1 2 3 4 5
DEVELOPING Total	_____

SHARING Your Life Mission Every Day

I am cultivating relationships with non-Christians and praying for God to give me natural opportunities to share his love.	1 2 3 4 5
I am praying and learning about where God can use me and our group cross-culturally for missions.	1 2 3 4 5
I am investing my time in another person or group who needs to know Christ.	1 2 3 4 5
I am regularly inviting unchurched or unconnected friends to my church or small group.	1 2 3 4 5
SHARING Total	_____

SURRENDERING Your Life for God's Pleasure

I am experiencing more of the presence and power of God in my everyday life.	1 2 3 4 5
I am faithfully attending services and my small group to worship God.	1 2 3 4 5
I am seeking to please God by surrendering every area of my life (health, decisions, finances, relationships, future, etc.) to him.	1 2 3 4 5
I am accepting the things I cannot change and becoming increasingly grateful for the life I've been given.	1 2 3 4 5
SURRENDERING Total	_____

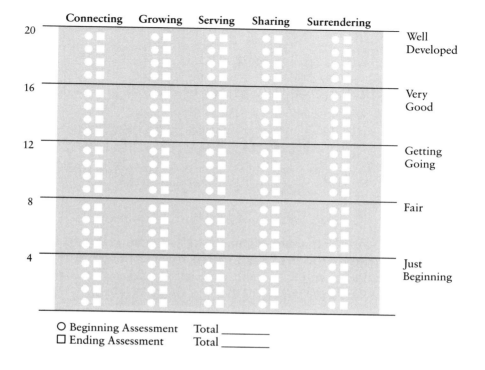

PERSONAL HEALTH PLAN

This worksheet could become your single most important feature in this study. On it you can record your personal priorities before the Father. It will help you live a healthy spiritual life, balancing all five of God's purposes.

PURPOSE	PLAN
CONNECT	WHO are you connecting with spiritually?
GROW	WHAT is your next step for growth?
DEVELOP	WHERE are you serving?
SHARE	WHEN are you shepherding another in Christ?
SURRENDER	HOW are you surrendering your heart to God?

DATE	MY PROGRESS	PARTNER'S PROGRESS

Personal Health Plan

DATE	MY PROGRESS	PARTNER'S PROGRESS

SAMPLE PERSONAL HEALTH PLAN

This worksheet could become your single most important feature in this study. On it you can record your personal priorities before the Father. It will help you live a healthy spiritual life, balancing all five of God's purposes.

PURPOSE	PLAN
CONNECT	WHO are you connecting with spiritually?
	Bill and I will meet weekly by e-mail or phone
GROW	WHAT is your next step for growth?
	Regular devotions or journaling my prayers 2×/week
DEVELOP	WHERE are you serving?
	Serving in children's ministry Go through GIFTS Assessment
SHARE	WHEN are you shepherding another in Christ?
	Shepherding Bill at lunch or hosting a starter group in the fall
SURRENDER	HOW are you surrendering your heart?
	Help with our teenager New job situation

DATE	MY PROGRESS	PARTNER'S PROGRESS
3/5	Talked during our group	Figured out our goals together
3/12	Missed our time together	Missed our time together
3/26	Met for coffee and review of my goals	Met for coffee
4/10	E-mailed prayer requests	Bill sent me his prayer requests
5/5	Great start on personal journaling	Read Mark 1–6 in one sitting!
5/12	Traveled and not doing well this week	Journaled about Christ as healer
5/26	Back on track	Busy and distracted; asked for prayer
6/1	Need to call Children's Pastor	
6/26	Group did a serving project together	Agreed to lead group worship
6/30	Regularly rotating leadership	Led group worship–great job!
7/5	Called Jim to see if he's open to joining our group	Wanted to invite somebody, but didn't
7/12	Preparing to start a group in fall	
7/30	Group prayed for me	Told friend something I'm learning about Christ
8/5	Overwhelmed but encouraged	Scared to lead worship
8/15	Felt heard and more settled	Issue with wife
8/30	Read book on teens	Glad he took on his fear

SPIRITUAL GIFTS INVENTORY

A spiritual gift is given to each of us as a means of helping the entire church.

1 Corinthians 12:7 (NLT)

A spiritual gift is a special ability, given by the Holy Spirit to every believer at their conversion. Although spiritual gifts are given when the Holy Spirit enters new believers, their use and purpose need to be understood and developed as we grow spiritually. A spiritual gift is much like a muscle; the more you use it, the stronger it becomes.

A Few Truths about Spiritual Gifts

1. Only believers have spiritual gifts. 1 Corinthians 2:14
2. You can't earn or work for a spiritual gift. Ephesians 4:7
3. The Holy Spirit decides what gifts I get. 1 Corinthians 12:11
4. I am to develop the gifts God gives me. Romans 11:29; 2 Timothy 1:6
5. It's a sin to waste the gifts God gave me. 1 Corinthians 4:1–2; Matthew 25:14–30
6. Using my gifts honors God and expands me. John 15:8

Gifts Inventory

God wants us to know what spiritual gift(s) he has given us. One person can have many gifts. The goal is to find the areas in which the Holy Spirit seems to have supernaturally empowered our service to others. These gifts are to be used to minister to others and build up the body of Christ.

There are four main lists of gifts found in the Bible in Romans 12:3–8; 1 Corinthians 12:1–11, 27–31; Ephesians 4:11–12; and 1 Peter 4:9–11. There are other passages that mention or illustrate gifts not included in these lists. As you read through this list, prayerfully consider whether the biblical definition describes you. Remember, you can have more than one gift, but everyone has at least one.

ADMINISTRATION (Organization)—1 Corinthians 12

This is the ability to recognize the gifts of others and recruit them to a ministry. It is the ability to organize and manage people, resources, and time for effective ministry.

APOSTLE—1 Corinthians 12

This is the ability to start new churches/ventures and oversee their development.

DISCERNMENT—1 Corinthians 12

This is the ability to distinguish between the spirit of truth and the spirit of error; to detect inconsistencies in another's life and confront in love.

ENCOURAGEMENT (Exhortation)—Romans 12

This is the ability to motivate God's people to apply and act on biblical principles, especially when they are discouraged or wavering in their faith. It is also the ability to bring out the best in others and challenge them to develop their potential.

EVANGELISM—Ephesians 4

This is the ability to communicate the gospel of Jesus Christ to unbelievers in a positive, nonthreatening way and to sense opportunities to share Christ and lead people to respond with faith.

FAITH—1 Corinthians 12

This is the ability to trust God for what cannot be seen and to act on God's promise, regardless of what the circumstances indicate. This includes a willingness to risk failure in pursuit of a God-given vision, expecting God to handle the obstacles.

GIVING—Romans 12

This is the ability to generously contribute material resources and/or money beyond the 10 percent tithe so that the church may grow and be strengthened. It includes the ability to manage money so it may be given to support the ministry of others.

HOSPITALITY—1 Peter 4:9–10

This is the ability to make others, especially strangers, feel warmly welcomed, accepted, and comfortable in the church family and the ability to coordinate factors that promote fellowship.

LEADERSHIP—Romans 12

This is the ability to clarify and communicate the purpose and direction ("vision") of a ministry in a way that attracts others to get involved, including the ability to motivate others, by example, to work together in accomplishing a ministry goal.

MERCY—Romans 12

This is the ability to manifest practical, compassionate, cheerful love toward suffering members of the body of Christ.

PASTORING (Shepherding)—Ephesians 4

This is the ability to care for the spiritual needs of a group of believers and equip them for ministry. It is also the ability to nurture a small group in spiritual growth and assume responsibility for their welfare.

PREACHING—Romans 12

This is the ability to publicly communicate God's Word in an inspired way that convinces unbelievers and both challenges and comforts believers.

SERVICE—Romans 12

This is the ability to recognize unmet needs in the church family, and take the initiative to provide practical assistance quickly, cheerfully, and without a need for recognition.

TEACHING—Ephesians 4

This is the ability to educate God's people by clearly explaining and applying the Bible in a way that causes them to learn; it is the ability to equip and train other believers for ministry.

WISDOM—1 Corinthians 12

This is the ability to understand God's perspective on life situations and share those insights in a simple, understandable way.

TELLING YOUR STORY

First, don't underestimate the power of your testimony. Revelation 12:11 says, "They have defeated [Satan] by the blood of the Lamb and by their testimony. And they did not love their lives so much that they were afraid to die" (NLT).

A simple three-point approach is very effective in communicating your personal testimony. The approach focuses on before you trusted Christ, how you surrendered to him, and the difference in you since you've been walking with him. If you became a Christian at a very young age and don't remember what life was like before Christ, reflect on what you have seen in the lives of others. Before you begin, pray and ask God to give you the right words.

Before You Knew Christ

Simply tell what your life was like before you surrendered to Christ. What was the key problem, emotion, situation, or attitude you were dealing with? What motivated you? What were your actions? How did you try to satisfy your inner needs? Create an interesting picture of your preconversion life and problems, and then explain what created a need and interest in Christian things.

How You Came to Know Christ

How were you converted? Simply tell the events and circumstances that caused you to consider Christ as the solution to your needs. Take time to identify the steps that brought you to the point of trusting Christ. Where were you? What was happening at the time? What people or problems influenced your decision?

The Difference Christ Has Made in Your Life

What is different about your life in Christ? How has his forgiveness impacted you? How have your thoughts, attitudes, and emotions changed? What problems have been resolved or changed? Share how Christ is meeting your needs and what a relationship with him means to you now. This should be the largest part of your story.

Tips

- Don't use jargon: don't sound churchy, preachy, or pious.
- Stick to the point. Your conversion and new life in Christ should be the main points.
- Be specific. Include events, genuine feelings, and personal insights, both before and after conversion, which people would be interested in and that clarify your main point. This makes your testimony easier to relate to. Assume you are sharing with someone with no knowledge of the Christian faith.
- Be current. Tell what is happening in your life with God now, today.
- Be honest. Don't exaggerate or portray yourself as living a perfect life with no problems. This is not realistic. The simple truth of what God has done in your life is all the Holy Spirit needs to convict someone of their sin and convince them of his love and grace.
- Remember, it's the Holy Spirit who convicts. You need only be obedient and tell your story.
- When people reply to your efforts to share with statements like "I don't believe in God," "I don't believe the Bible is God's Word," or "How can a loving God allow suffering?" how can we respond to these replies?

- Above all, keep a positive attitude. Don't be defensive.
- Be sincere. This will speak volumes about your confidence in your faith.
- Don't be offended. It's not you they are rejecting.
- Pray—silently on-the-spot. Don't proceed without asking for God's help about the specific question. Seek his guidance on how, or if, you should proceed at this time.
- In God's wisdom, choose to do one of the following:
  - Postpone sharing at this time.
  - Answer their objections, if you can.
  - Promise to research their questions and return answers later.

Step 1. Everywhere Jesus went he used stories, or parables, to demonstrate our need for salvation. Through these stories, he helped people see the error of their ways, leading them to turn to him. Your story can be just as powerful today. Begin to develop your story by sharing what your life was like before you knew Christ. (If you haven't yet committed your life to Christ, or became a Christian at a very young age and don't remember what life was like before Christ, reflect on what you have seen in the life of someone close to you.) Make notes about this aspect of your story below and commit to writing it out this week.

_____

_____

_____

Step 2. Sit in groups of two or three people for this discussion. Review the "How You Came to Know Christ" section. Begin to develop this part of your story by sharing within your circle. Make notes about this aspect of your story below and commit to writing it out this week.

_____

_____

_____

Step 2b. Connecting: Go around the group and share about a time you were stopped cold while sharing Christ, by a question you couldn't answer. What happened?

Step 2c. Sharing: Previously we talked about the questions and objections we receive that stop us from continuing to share our faith with someone. These questions/objections might include:

- "I don't believe in God."
- "I don't believe the Bible is God's Word."
- "How can a loving God allow suffering?"

How can we respond to these replies?

Step 3. Subgroup into groups of two or three people for this discussion. Review "The Difference Christ Has Made in Your Life" section. Share the highlights of this part of your story within your circle. Make notes about this aspect of your story below and commit to writing it out this week.

_____

_____

_____

Step 3b. Story: There's nothing more exciting than a brand-new believer. My wife became a Christian four years before I met her. She was a flight attendant at the time. Her zeal to introduce others to Jesus was reminiscent of the woman at the well who ran and got the whole town out to see Jesus.

My wife immediately began an international organization of Christian flight attendants for fellowship and for reaching out to others in their profession. She organized events where many people came to Christ, and bid for trips with another flight attendant who was a Christian so they could witness on the planes. They even bid for the shorter trips so they could talk to as many different people as possible. They had a goal for every flight to talk to at least one person about Christ, and to be encouraged by at least one person who already knew him. God met that request every time.

In her zeal, however, she went home to her family over the holidays and vacations and had little or no success. Later she would realize that she pressed them too hard. Jesus said a prophet is without honor in his own town, and I think the same goes for family. That's because members of your family think they know you, and are more likely to ignore changes, choosing instead to see you as they've always seen you. "Isn't this the carpenter's son—the son of Joseph?" they said of Jesus. "Don't we know this guy?"

With family members you have to walk with Christ openly and be patient. Change takes time. And remember, we don't save anyone. We just introduce them to Jesus through telling our own story. God does the rest.

Step 4. As a group, review *Telling Your Story*. Share which part of your story is the most difficult for you to tell. Which is the easiest for you? If you have time, a few of you share your story with the group.

Step 5. Throughout this study we have had the opportunity to develop our individual testimonies. One way your group can serve each other is to provide a safe forum for "practicing" telling your stories. Continue to take turns sharing your testimonies now. Set a time limit—say two to three minutes each. Don't miss this great opportunity to get to know one another better and encourage each other's growth too.

SERVING COMMUNION

Churches vary in their treatment of communion (or the Lord's Supper). We offer one simple form by which a small group can share this experience together. You can adapt this as necessary, or omit it from your group altogether, depending on your church's beliefs.

Steps in Serving Communion

1. Open by sharing about God's love, forgiveness, grace, mercy, commitment, tenderheartedness, faithfulness, etc., out of your personal journey (connect with the stories of those in the room).
2. Read one or several of the passages listed below.
3. Pray and pass the bread around the circle.
4. When everyone has been served, remind them that this represents Jesus's broken body on their behalf. Simply state, "Jesus said, 'Do this in remembrance of me' (Luke 22:19 NIV). Let us eat together," and eat the bread as a group.
5. Then read the rest of the passage: "In the same way, after the supper he took the cup, saying, 'This cup is the new covenant in my blood, which is poured out for you'" (Luke 22:20 NIV).
6. Pray, and serve the cups, either by passing a small tray, serving them individually, or having members pick up a cup from the table.
7. When everyone has been served, remind them the juice represents Christ's blood shed for them, then simply state, "Take and drink in remembrance of him. Let us drink together."
8. Finish by singing a simple song, listening to a praise song, or having a time of prayer in thanks to God.

Communion passages: Matthew 26:26–29; Mark 14:22–25; Luke 22:14–20; 1 Corinthians 10:16–21; 11:17–34.

PERFORMING A FOOTWASHING

Scripture: John 13:1–17. Jesus makes it quite clear to his disciples that his position as the Father's Son includes being a servant rather than power and glory only. To properly understand the scene and the intention of Jesus, we must realize that the washing of feet was the duty of slaves and indeed of non-Jewish rather than Jewish slaves. Jesus placed himself in the position of a servant. He displayed to the disciples self-sacrifice and love. In view of his majesty, only the symbolic position of a slave was adequate to open their eyes and keep them from lofty illusions. The point of footwashing, then, is to correct the attitude that Jesus discerned in the disciples. It constitutes the permanent basis for mutual service, service in your group and for the community around you, which is the responsibility of all Christians.

When to Implement

There are three primary places we would recommend you insert a footwashing: during a break in the Surrendering section of your group; during a break in the Growing section of your group; or at the closing of your group. A special time of prayer for each person as he or she gets his or her feet washed can be added to the footwashing time.

SURRENDERING AT THE CROSS

Surrendering everything to God is one of the most challenging aspects of following Jesus. It involves a relationship built on trust and faith. Each of us is in a different place on our spiritual journey. Some of us have known the Lord for many years, some are new in our faith, and some may still be checking God out. Regardless, we all have things that we still want control over—things we don't want to give to God because we don't know what he will do with them. These things are truly more important to us than God is—they have become our god.

We need to understand that God wants us to be completely devoted to him. If we truly love God with all our heart, soul, strength, and mind (Luke 10:27), we will be willing to give him everything.

Steps in Surrendering at the Cross

1. You will need some small pieces of paper and pens or pencils for people to write down the things they want to sacrifice/surrender to God.
2. If you have a wooden cross, hammers, and nails you can have the members nail their sacrifices to the cross. If you don't have a wooden cross, get creative. Think of another way to symbolically relinquish the sacrifices to God. You might use a fireplace to burn them in the fire as an offering to the Lord. The point is giving to the Lord whatever hinders your relationship with him.

3. Create an atmosphere conducive to quiet reflection and prayer. Whatever this quiet atmosphere looks like for your group, do the best you can to create a peaceful time to meet with God.
4. Once you are settled, prayerfully think about the points below. Let the words and thoughts draw you into a heart-to-heart connection with your Lord Jesus Christ.

☐ *Worship him.* Ask God to change your viewpoint so you can worship him through a surrendered spirit.

☐ *Humble yourself.* Surrender doesn't happen without humility. James 4:6–7 says: "'God opposes the proud but gives grace to the humble.' Submit yourselves, then, to God" (NIV).

☐ *Surrender your mind, will, and emotions.* This is often the toughest part of surrendering. What do you sense God urging you to give him so you can have the kind of intimacy he desires with you? Our hearts yearn for this kind of connection with him; let go of the things that stand between you.

☐ *Write out your prayer.* Write out your prayer of sacrifice and surrender to the Lord. This may be an attitude, a fear, a person, a job, a possession—anything that God reveals is a hindrance to your relationship with him.

5. After writing out your sacrifice, take it to the cross and offer it to the Lord. Nail your sacrifice to the cross, or burn it as a sacrifice in the fire.
6. Close by singing, praying together, or taking communion. Make this time as short or as long as seems appropriate for your group.

Surrendering to God is life-changing and liberating. God desires that we be overcomers! First John 4:4 says, "You, dear children, are from God and have overcome . . . because the one who is in you is greater than the one who is in the world" (NIV).

JOURNALING 101

Henri Nouwen says effective and lasting ministry *for* God grows out of a quiet place alone *with* God. This is why journaling is so important.

The greatest adventure of our lives is found in the daily pursuit of knowing, growing in, serving, sharing, and worshiping Christ forever. This is the essence of a purposeful life: to see all these biblical purposes fully formed and balanced in our lives. Only then are we "complete in Christ" (Col. 1:28 NASB).

David poured his heart out to God by writing psalms. The book of Psalms contains many of his honest conversations with God in written form, including expressions of every imaginable emotion on every aspect of his life. Like David, we encourage you to select a strategy to integrate God's Word and journaling into your devotional time. Use any of the following resources:

- Bible
- Bible reading plan
- Devotional
- Topical Bible study plan

Before and after you read a portion of God's Word, speak to God in honest reflection in the form of a written prayer. You may begin this time by simply finishing the sentence "Father, . . . ," "Yesterday, Lord, . . . ," or "Thank you, God, for, ..." Share with him where you are at the present moment; express your hurts, disappointments, frustrations, blessings, victories, and gratefulness. Whatever you do with your journal, make a plan that fits you, so you'll have a positive experience. Consider sharing highlights of your progress and experiences with some or all of your group members, especially your spiritual partner. You may find they want to join and even encourage you in this journey. Most of all, enjoy the ride and cultivate a more authentic, growing walk with God.

PRAYER AND PRAISE REPORT

Briefly share your prayer requests with the large group, making notations below. Then gather in small groups of two to four to pray for each other.

Date: _____

Prayer Requests

_____
_____
_____
_____
_____

Praise Reports

_____
_____
_____
_____
_____

Prayer and Praise Report

Briefly share your prayer requests with the large group, making notations below. Then gather in small groups of two to four to pray for each other.

Date: _____

Prayer Requests

_____

_____

_____

_____

_____

Praise Reports

_____

_____

_____

_____

_____

Prayer and Praise Report

Briefly share your prayer requests with the large group, making notations below. Then gather in small groups of two to four to pray for each other.

Date: _____

Prayer Requests

_____

_____

_____

_____

_____

Praise Reports

_____

_____

_____

_____

_____

Prayer and Praise Report

Briefly share your prayer requests with the large group, making notations below. Then gather in small groups of two to four to pray for each other.

Date: _____

Prayer Requests

_____

_____

_____

_____

_____

Praise Reports

_____

_____

_____

_____

_____

Prayer and Praise Report

Briefly share your prayer requests with the large group, making notations below. Then gather in small groups of two to four to pray for each other.

Date: _____

Prayer Requests

_____

_____

_____

_____

_____

Praise Reports

_____

_____

_____

_____

_____

SMALL GROUP ROSTER

Name	Address	Phone	E-mail Address	Team or Role	When/How to Contact You
Bill Jones	7 Alvalar Street L.F. 92665	766-2255	bjones@aol.com	Socials	Evenings After 5

(Pass your book around your group at your first meeting to get everyone's name and contact information.)

Name	Address	Phone	E-mail Address	Team or Role	When/How to Contact You

LEADING FOR THE FIRST TIME
LEADERSHIP 101

Sweaty palms are a healthy sign. The Bible says God is gracious to the humble. Remember who is in control; the time to worry is when you're not worried. Those who are soft in heart (and sweaty-palmed) are those whom God is sure to speak through.

Seek support. Ask your leader, coleader, or close friend to pray for you and prepare with you before the session. Walking through the study will help you anticipate potentially difficult questions and discussion topics.

Bring your uniqueness to the study. Lean into who you are and how God wants you to uniquely lead the study.

Prepare. Prepare. Prepare. Go through the session several times. If you are using the DVD, listen to the teaching segment and *Leader Lifter*. Consider writing in a journal or fasting for a day to prepare yourself for what God wants to do.

Don't wait until the last minute to prepare.

Ask for feedback so you can grow. Perhaps in an e-mail or on cards handed out at the study, have everyone write down three things you did well and one thing you could improve on. Don't get defensive, but show an openness to learn and grow.

Prayerfully consider launching a new group. This doesn't need to happen overnight, but God's heart is for this to happen over time. Not all Christians are called to be leaders or teachers, but we are all called to be "shepherds" of a few someday.

Share with your group what God is doing in your heart. God is searching for those whose hearts are fully his. Share your trials and victories. We promise that people will relate.

Prayerfully consider whom you would like to pass the baton to next week. It's only fair. God is ready for the next member of your group to go on the faith journey you just traveled. Make it fun, and expect God to do the rest.

LEADER'S NOTES
INTRODUCTION

Congratulations! You have responded to the call to help shepherd Jesus's flock. There are few other tasks in the family of God that surpass the contribution you will be making. We have provided you several ways to prepare for this role. Between the *Read Me First*, these *Leader's Notes*, and the *Watch This First* and *Leader Lifter* segments on the optional *Deepening Life Together: Revelation* Video Teaching DVD, you'll have all you need to do a great job of leading your group. Just don't forget, you are not alone. God knew that you would be asked to lead this group and he won't let you down. In Hebrews 13:5b God promises us, "Never will I leave you; never will I forsake you" (NIV).

Your role as leader is to create a safe, warm environment for your group. As a leader, your most important job is to create an atmosphere where people are willing to talk honestly about what the topics discussed in this study have to do with them. Be available before people arrive so you can greet them at the door. People are naturally nervous at a new group, so a hug or handshake can help put them at ease. Before you start leading your group, a little preparation will give you confidence. Review the *Read Me First* at the front of your study guide so you'll understand the purpose of each section, enabling you to help your group understand it as well.

If you're new to leading a group, congratulations and thank you; this will be a life-changing experience for you also. We have provided these *Leader's Notes* to help new leaders begin well.

It's important in your first meeting to make sure group members understand that things shared personally and in prayer must remain confidential. Also, be careful not to dominate the group discussion, but facilitate it and encourage others to join in and share. And lastly, have fun.

Take a moment at the beginning of your first meeting to orient the group to one principle that undergirds this study: A healthy small group balances the purposes of the church. Most small groups emphasize Bible study, fellowship, and prayer. But God has called us to reach out to others as well. He wants us to do what Jesus teaches, not just learn about it.

Preparing for each meeting ahead of time. Take the time to review the session, the *Leader's Notes*, and *Leader Lifter* for the session before each session. Also write down your answers to each question. Pay special attention to exercises that ask group members to *do* something. These exercises will help your group live out what the Bible teaches, not just talk about it. Be sure you understand how the exercises work, and bring any supplies you might need, such as paper or pens. Pray for your group members by name at least once between sessions and before each session. Use the *Prayer and Praise Report* so you will remember their prayer requests. Ask God to use your time together to touch the heart of every person. Expect God to give you the opportunity to talk with those he wants you to encourage or challenge in a special way.

Don't try to go it alone. Pray for God to help you. Ask other members of your group to help by taking on some small role. In the *Appendix* you'll find the *Team Roles* pages with some suggestions to get people involved. Leading is more rewarding if you give group members opportunities to help. Besides, helping group members discover their individual gifts for serving or even leading the group will bless all of you.

Consider asking a few people to come early to help set up, pray, and introduce newcomers to others. Even if everyone is new, they don't know that yet and may be shy when they arrive. You might give people roles like setting up name tags or handing out drinks. This could be a great way to spot a co-leader.

Subgrouping. If your group has more than seven people, break into discussion groups of three to four people for the *Growing* and *Surrendering* sections each week. People will connect more with the study and each other when they have more opportunity to participate. Smaller discussion circles encourage quieter people to talk more and tend to minimize the effects of more vocal or dominant members. Also, people who are unaccustomed to praying aloud will feel more comfortable praying within a smaller group of people. Share prayer requests in the larger group and then break into smaller groups to pray for each other. People are more willing to pray in small circles if they know that the whole group will hear all the prayer requests.

Memorizing Scripture. At the start of each session you will find a memory verse—a verse for the group to memorize each week. Encourage your group members to do this. Memorizing God's Word is both directed and celebrated throughout the Bible, either explicitly ("Your word I have hidden in my heart, that I might not sin against You" [Ps. 119:11 NKJV]), or implicitly, as in the example of our Lord ("He departed to the mountain to pray" [Mark 6:46 NKJV]).

Anyone who has memorized Scripture can confirm the amazing spiritual benefits that result from this practice. Don't miss out on the opportunity to encourage your group to grow in the knowledge of God's Word through Scripture memorization.

Reflections. We've provided opportunity for a personal time with God using the *Reflections* at the end of each session. Don't press seekers to do this, but just remind the group that every believer should have a plan for personal time with God.

Inviting new people. Cast the vision, as Jesus did, to be inclusive not exclusive. Ask everyone to prayerfully think of people who would enjoy or benefit from a group like this—then invite them. The beginning of a new study is a great time to welcome a few people into your circle. Don't worry about ending up with too many people—you can always have one discussion circle in the living room and another in the dining room.

For Deeper Study (Optional). We have included a *For Deeper Study* section in each session. *For Deeper Study* provides additional passages for individual study on the topic of each session. If your group likes to do deeper Bible study, consider having members study the *For Deeper Study* passages for homework. Then, during the *Growing* portion of your meeting, you can share the high points of what you've learned.

LEADER'S NOTES
SESSIONS

Session One Setting: Audience and the Revealer

Connecting

1. We've designed this study for both new and established groups, and for both seekers and the spiritually mature. New groups will need to invest more time building relationships with each other. Established groups often want to dig deeper into Bible study and application. Regardless of whether your group is new or has been together for a while, be sure to answer this introductory question at this first session.

2. A very important item in this first session is the *Small Group Agreement*. An agreement helps clarify your group's priorities and cast new vision for what the group can become. You can find this in the *Appendix* of this study guide. We've found that groups that talk about these values up front and commit to an agreement benefit significantly. They work through conflicts long before people get to the point of frustration, so there's a lot less pain.

   Take some time to review this agreement before your meeting. Then during your meeting, read the agreement aloud to the entire group. If some people have concerns about a specific item or the agreement as a whole, be sensitive to their concerns. Explain that tens of thousands of groups use agreements like this one as a simple tool for building trust and group health over time.

   We recommend talking about shared ownership of the group. It's important that each member have a role. See the *Appendix* to learn more about *Team Roles*. This is a great tool to get this important practice launched in your group.

Growing

   This session covers Revelation 1. Reading the entire selection aloud may be time-consuming so we recommend that you ask the group to read these passages at home before coming to the group. Remember to be sensitive to those who are not comfortable reading aloud in a group.

4. Jesus is giving to John the revelation that God gave him. His purpose is to show his servants what must soon take place. John claims that the authority for this book comes straight from Jesus.

5. John was one of many persecuted believers who were partners in suffering as persecution escalated at the end of the first century AD. He was also a partner with other believers in God's coming kingdom because, as believers, they were already citizens of the kingdom. And they were partners in patient endurance as they awaited the arrival of God's coming kingdom. John had paid for his faithfulness in preaching the word of God and speaking about Jesus by being exiled to the island of Patmos. The Romans used Patmos as a place to banish political prisoners.

6. This question is designed to encourage people to discuss what John was going through as he received this revelation from God. Many interpreters believe he was transported (either physically or spiritually) out of the natural world to a Holy Spirit-empowered experience beyond the normal—he was not just dreaming.

7. Refer to the verses noted in the chart as you discuss each one. The word used here for robe is most frequently used to depict the garment worn by the high priest, one who goes into God's presence to obtain forgiveness of sin for those who have believed in him. The golden sash completes this priestly picture. His hair like white wool, like snow, indicates his wisdom and divine nature (see Dan. 7:9). His eyes like fire symbolize deep insight over the churches and the entire course of history (see 2:18; 19:12) and judgment over evil (see Dan. 10:6). The feet like bronze is a picture of a person with great power—exalted. Bronze usually symbolized the might of Rome. The voice like the sound of rushing waters (see 19:6) evokes the image of a voice so powerful and awesome that, when it speaks with authority, nothing else can be heard. The seven stars are explained in Revelation 1:20: "The mystery of the seven stars that you saw in my right hand and of the seven golden lampstands is this: The seven stars are the angels of the seven churches, and the seven lampstands are the seven churches" (NIV) to whom this letter is addressed. That Christ is holding the stars implies his protection of these churches as he walks among them. The double-edged sword was sharp on both edges. These swords gave a great advantage in hand-to-hand combat. This sword coming from Jesus's mouth symbolizes the power and force of his message. Jesus's words of judgment are as sharp as swords; he is completely invincible. The face brilliant like the sun probably describes Christ's entire being—his glory. The same picture is described in the Transfiguration—an event John witnessed (Matt. 17:2).

Jesus's appearance encompasses all parts of God's plan for humanity. His appearance also shows that he is the only one worthy to deliver God's message to John, as he embodies power, strength, authority, knowledge, wisdom, and so on.

8. John falls down at Jesus's feet, as though dead. This is the appropriate response to seeing the glory of God. The first thing Christ says to John is the same thing he said to the women at the tomb: "Don't be afraid!" (Matt. 28:5 NLT). There is no need for believers to fear. Jesus then identifies himself as the beginning and end of everything (see Isa. 44:6). He is also the living one—not a dead idol but resurrected, alive, and always with his people. He died—experienced physical death on the cross—but now is alive. Because Jesus rose from the dead, he can promise the same for his people. Death has no power over him (he holds the keys), so it should have no fear for believers. This was something significant to say to believers facing death for their faith.

9. This passage promises that God will bless the reader of this book. In addition to the reader, God blesses all who listen to it and obey what it says. "Listen" and "obey" are important terms and major themes of the book. The blessed ones are those who hear God's word and then obey it so that it changes their lives (Eph. 4:13). These words will bless the hearers because through them they can get to know God better and be able to trust him more completely.

No one knows when the prophecy in Revelation will come to pass, but Jesus assures us that it will be soon. Thus we should be prepared and remain ready for his return at any time.

Developing

This section enables you to help the group see the importance of developing their abilities for service to God.

10. The intent of this discussion is to encourage group members to set aside some time to spend with God in prayer and his Word at home each day throughout the week. Read through this section and be prepared to help the group understand how important it is to fill our minds with the Word of God. If people already have a commitment to a good Bible reading plan, that is great, but you may have people who struggle to stay in the Word daily. Sometimes beginning with a simple commitment to a short daily reading can start a habit that changes their life.

The *Reflections* pages at the end of each session include verses that were either talked about in the session or support the teaching of the session. They are very short readings with a few lines to encourage people to write down their thoughts. Remind the group about these *Reflections* each week after the *Surrendering* section. Encourage the group to see the importance of making this time to connect with God a priority in their life. Encourage them to commit to a next step in prayer, Bible reading, or meditation on the Word.

Suggested exercise: To help the group get started with meditating on the Word of God, consider providing everyone with a 3×5 index card. Have everyone write this week's memory verse on the card and begin memorizing Scripture together.

Sharing

Jesus wants all of his disciples to help outsiders connect with him, to know him personally. This section should provide an opportunity to go beyond Bible study to biblical living.

11. This activity should get the group to observe their interactions during the coming week with the intention of using these observations next week in evaluating the people that God has placed in their lives that he might want them to share with or invite to small group.

Surrendering

God is most pleased by a heart that is fully his. Each group session will provide group members a chance to surrender their hearts to God in prayer and worship. Group prayer requests and prayer time should be included every week.

12. Encourage group members to use the *Reflections* verses in their daily quiet time throughout the week. This will move them closer to God while reinforcing the lesson of this session through study of related Scripture.

13. As you move to a time of sharing prayer requests, be sure to remind the group of the importance of confidentiality and keeping what is shared in the group within the group. Everyone must feel that the personal things they share will be kept in confidence if you are to have safety and bonding within the group members.

For Deeper Study

We have included an optional *For Deeper Study* section in each session. *For Deeper Study* provides additional passages for individual study on the topic of each session. If your group likes to do deeper Bible study, consider having members study the *For Deeper Study* passages at home between meetings.

Session Two Suffering Believers

Connecting

2. We encourage the group to rotate leaders and host homes each meeting. This practice will go a long way toward bonding the group. Review the *Small Group Calendar* and talk about who else is willing to open their home or facilitate a meeting. Rotating host homes and leadership along with implementing *Team Roles* as discussed in *Session One* will quickly move the group ownership from "your group" to "our group."

Growing

4. He is the First and the Last, who died and came to life again (2:8). He triumphed over death, and the saints need to know this so that his triumph can help those who are being tempted to give up their faith under pressure.

   He is the one whose words are holy and true and who holds the key of David (the key to David's royal palace, 3:7). Jesus is the only one in history who provides access to the presence of God and so reveals what is truth.

6. The church at Smyrna is suffering affliction and poverty and is about to experience persecution from the devil for a period of ten days (perhaps a symbolic description of some local persecution); some will be imprisoned, but they must be faithful even to the point of death.

   Philadelphia has little strength (political influence), but Jesus has placed before them an open door (an opportunity for bold witness) because they have kept Jesus's word and have not denied his name.

   Christians in many parts of the world are suffering similarly. An Internet search could produce several news stories that might help bring this part of Revelation alive for your group members.

7. Jesus promises the church in Smyrna that even if they suffer physical death, he will reward them with eternal life and the victor's crown.

   Jesus promises the church in Philadelphia that they will not only be welcome in God's house but will be vital, weight-bearing parts of God's house.

8. God takes his relationships with his people seriously. He sees what is happening in our lives and instructs us in difficult situations. He wants us to have a relationship with him and he tells us how we can do this.

Developing

10. For many, spiritual partners will be a new idea. We highly encourage you to try pairs for this study. It's so hard to start a spiritual practice like prayer or consistent Bible reading with no support. A friend makes a huge difference. As leader, you may want to prayerfully decide who would be a good match with whom. Remind people that this partnership isn't forever; it's just for a few weeks. Be sure to have extra copies of the *Personal Health Plan* available at this meeting in case you need to have a group of three spiritual partners. It is a good idea for you to look over the *Personal Health Plan* before the meeting so you can help people understand how to use it.

    Instruct your group members to enlist a spiritual partner by asking them to pair up with someone in the group (we suggest that men partner with men and women with women) and turn to the *Personal Health Plan* in the *Appendix*.

    Ask the group to complete the instructions in the session for the WHO and WHAT questions on the *Personal Health Plan*. Your group has now begun to address two of God's purposes for their lives!

    You can see that the *Personal Health Plan* contains space to record the ups and downs and progress each week in the column labeled "My Progress." When partners check in each week, they can record their partner's progress in the goal he or she chose in the "Partner's Progress" column on this chart. In the *Appendix* you'll find a *Sample Personal Health Plan* filled in as an example.

    The WHERE, WHEN, and HOW questions on the *Personal Health Plan* will be addressed in future sessions of the study.

Sharing

12. A *Circles of Life* diagram is provided for you and the group to use to help you identify people who need a connection to Christian community. Encourage the group to commit to praying for God's guidance and an opportunity to reach out to each person in their *Circles of Life*.

    We encourage this outward focus for your group because groups that become too inwardly focused tend to become unhealthy over time. People naturally gravitate toward feeding themselves through Bible study, prayer, and social time, so it's usually up to the leader to push them to consider how this inward nourishment can overflow into outward concern for others. Never forget: Jesus came to seek and save the lost and to find a shepherd for every sheep.

    Talk to the group about the importance of inviting people; remind them that healthy small groups make a habit of inviting friends, neighbors, unconnected church members, co-workers, etc., to join their groups or join them at a weekend service. When people get connected to a group of new friends, they often join the church.

Some groups are happy with the people they already have in the group and they don't really want to grow larger. Some fear that newcomers will interrupt the intimacy that members have built over time. However, groups generally gain strength with the infusion of new people. It's like a river of living water flowing into a stagnant pond. Some groups remain permanently open, while others open periodically, such as at the beginning and ending of a study. If your circle becomes too large for easy face-to-face conversations, you can simply form a second or third discussion circle in another room in your home.

Surrendering

13. Be sure to remind the group of the importance of confidentiality and keeping what is shared in the group within the group. Use the *Prayer and Praise Report* to record your prayer requests.

14. Last week we talked briefly about incorporating *Reflections* into the group members' daily time with God. Some people don't yet have an established quiet time. With this in mind, engage a discussion with the group about the importance of making daily time with God a priority. Talk about potential obstacles and practical ideas for how to overcome them. The *Reflections* verses could serve as a springboard for drawing near to God. So don't forget these are a valuable resource for your group.

Session Three Compromising Churches

Connecting

1. Encourage group members to take time to complete the *Personal Health Assessment*. In the next question you will have the opportunity to pair up spiritual partners to discuss one thing that is going well and one thing that needs work. Participants should not be asked to share any aspect of this assessment in the large group if they don't want to.

Growing

4. Sharp, double-edged sword: The Lord will judge those who continue to sin and do not repent.
   Eyes blazing fire: Jesus discerns the sinners from the pure-hearted.
   Feet burnished bronze: He is filled with strength, the strength to repay humanity according to its deeds.

Word of the One who holds the seven spirits of God: Jesus's sovereignty is perfect.

Words of the Amen, etc.: Jesus is the true Son of God, the ruler of God's creation. There is no other than him.

6. Repentance is basic, critical. These churches need the consistent, balanced, healthy teaching of God's Word and the obedience to that Word. If people will not repent, Christ's saving Word will become their judge. The implication of this is that if a person who claims to be a Christian and lives an immoral lifestyle or a compromising belief system without repenting—that person will experience God's judgment.

7. The only cure for lukewarmness is fresh opening of our hearts to Jesus Christ. He invites us to invite him in to an intimate relationship and walk with him. Opening ourselves to intimacy with Jesus is something we need to do constantly, not just once when we are saved.

Developing

9. Group members who are currently serving the body of Christ in some capacity should be encouraged to share their experiences with the group as a way to encourage them. All group members should consider where they could take a next step toward getting involved in ministry. Discuss some of the ministries that your church may offer to people looking to get involved, such as the children's ministry, ushering, or hospitality. Remind everyone that it sometimes takes time and trying several different ministries before finding the one that fits best.

Sharing

11. It is important to return to the *Circles of Life* and encourage the group to follow through in their commitments to invite people who need to know Christ more deeply through Christian community. When people are asked why they never go to church they often say, "No one ever invited me." Remind the group that our responsibility is to invite people, but it is the Holy Spirit's responsibility to compel them to come.

Session Four Worship in Heaven

Growing

This session covers Revelation 4–5. Reading the entire selection aloud may be time-consuming so we recommend that you ask the group to read these passages at home before coming to the group.

3. John is standing before an open door in heaven. He is then taken in the Spirit to the throne room. God's appearance is jewel-like, shining in brilliant-colored light, magnificent, beautiful.

6. The twenty-four elders, who are considered royalty in their own right, fall down before the Lord, lay their crowns before the throne, and worship him. He is the highest of the high, the most worthy of all. This is an example of how we will someday approach God.

7. John weeps because there is no one worthy to take the scroll from the right hand of God. This scroll will have great implication as we go through the book of Revelation—all the seals will be unloosed and the judgments will come. In the end it is this scroll in the right hand of God that, once loosed, brings the kingdom of heaven. The scroll is something like the title deed to the world, or the book of the inheritance of the King's sons and daughters. The only one worthy to open the book is the one who died to win those who will inherit the kingdom. He is both the royal Lion descended from King David and the sacrificed Lamb.

8. Jesus is the Lamb, who was sacrificed for our sins. The Lamb is the only one worthy to take the scroll and open its seals because of the sacrifice he made for humanity—dying for their sins. Calling him the Lamb reminds us of the Passover when the people were to select a lamb—not any lamb, but one special lamb chosen for its perfection and beauty—to be sacrificed to the Lord. Jesus is our Passover lamb. He has bought, purchased, and redeemed us and the entire earth. The seven horns and eyes suggest the fullness of power and wisdom of the sevenfold Spirit.

9. A gathering of countless people is standing in front of the throne and the Lamb, singing praises to God and Jesus. The Lamb, together with God, is worthy of this extravagant glory and praise.

Developing

12. This activity provides an opportunity for the group to share the love of Jesus by meeting real, felt needs. Discuss this with everyone and choose one action step to take as a group. Be certain that everyone understands his or her role in this activity. It might be a good idea to call each person during the week to be sure they don't forget to bring to the next session what is required of them.

    Designate one person to investigate where to donate items in your area. That person can also be responsible for dropping off the items.

13. Point the group to the *Spiritual Gifts Inventory*. Read through the spiritual gifts and engage the group in discussion about which gifts they believe they have. Encourage them to review these further on their own time during the

coming week, giving prayerful consideration to each one. We will refer back to this again later in the study.

Sharing

15. Encourage group members to consider developing their salvation story as a tool for sharing their faith with others. Begin the process during your group time and encourage the group to complete the exercise at home. As leader, you should review the "Tips" section of *Telling Your Story* yourself in advance and be ready to share your ideas about this process with the group.

Session Five Judgment

Growing

This session covers Revelation 6 and 8–11. Reading the entire selection aloud may be time-consuming so we recommend that you ask the group to read these passages at home before coming to the group.

4. God must avenge evil and administer consequences for those who deserve it. He has provided ample time for people to change their ways, and he has provided a generous alternative to judgment: forgiveness through faith in the Lamb, who has personally suffered the full penalty, although he is innocent. This combination of mercy (sparing the repentant) and judgment (punishing evil) reveal his divine justice.

5. These souls were murdered because of their belief in Christ. Sometimes we wonder why God doesn't do something drastic about evil. Revelation shows God doing something drastic.

6. This is a short period of time to anticipate the grim reality of the judgments God is about to unleash.

7. One third of the earth, sea, rivers, and the moon and stars are destroyed. The significance of one third is probably that only a portion is destroyed and so the judgment is not yet complete. There is more to come.

8. The locust-scorpions are to torture for five months those who don't have the seal of God. They spare those who do have the seal of God, as well as the trees, grass, and plants.

9. Answers may vary, but possibilities include unbelief, pride, love of evil and iniquity, and Satan's deception. It's astonishing how people cling to their beliefs and habits.

10. There is a swiftness with which each judgment is poured out. After the bowls are emptied on the earth, the Second Coming of Christ will be ushered in. A great calamity will ensue with a great earthquake which splits the great city into three parts and makes all other cities collapse.

11. The elders praise God for his judgment of the wicked and the mercy he bestows on the believers.

12. Revelation 6:9–11: the souls of those who had been slain
Revelation 7:4–8: the 144,000
Revelation 7:9–17: the great multitude in white robes
Revelation 11:3–12: the two witnesses

13. The purpose of judgments is to bring forth repentance so God can bless those who repent. It is to stop evil and change the hearts of evildoers. Jesus said, "I have come that they might have life" (John 10:10 NIV). When we turn our backs on God, there are consequences—for us and the world. We are warned with each succeeding judgment. Repent—a greater judgment is coming. The judgments are all about bringing a final end to evil in the world.

Developing

16. Encourage group members to use the *Personal Health Plan* to jot down their next step to serving in ministry, with a plan for how and when they will begin.

Sharing

17. This activity provides an opportunity for the group to share Jesus in a very practical way. Discuss this with everyone and choose one action step to take as a group. Be certain that everyone understands his or her role in this activity. It might be a good idea to call each person during the week to be sure they don't forget to bring to the next session what is required of them.

   Designate one person to investigate where to donate items in your area. That person can also be responsible for dropping off the items.

Session Six Persecution

Growing

5. It's important for us to know that one of Satan's main tactics is to accuse us, either inside our heads or through the mouths of others. He wants to shame us, silence us, paralyze us from saying and doing what God has given

us to do in the world. He wants to keep us from testifying to the world about who God is and what he has done for us. The brothers triumph over him first through something they receive by sheer grace: Jesus's shed blood that wins forgiveness for their sins. They can thus ignore Satan's accusations about how bad they are. They also triumph over him by continuing to testify, even if that means death. Most of us hope we never have to face that choice: death or witnessing for Christ. But most of us could use a lot more courage in speaking up for Christ and doing his work in the world. Many of us tend to love our lives too much.

6. They're surrounded by people worshiping evil, and they face pressure to do the same—threats of arrest or death. They endure a terribly repressive government and hideous blasphemies against God. They're told they can't buy or sell anything unless they accept the mark of Satan's representative. To endure in such times it takes tremendous courage, clarity about who God is (in the face of confusing counter-messages), and confidence that God is good and will ultimately triumph. While this tribulation may be the worst ever, Christians have faced similar circumstances in many periods. Two examples are the Soviet Union, and China during its Cultural Revolution.

Developing

9. This activity provides an opportunity for the group to share Jesus in a very practical way. Discuss this with the group and choose one action step to take as a group. Invite one person to volunteer to be the point person on this. They would investigate the action step you have chosen and report back to the group what they find out next week. For example, if you have chosen to do yard work, then the point person would contact the church to find a needy family and schedule the work to be done. It is ideal that every member of the group participates, but don't wait until all schedules align before making a plan to follow through. Many times, waiting until eight or ten individuals are available can cause a plan to fizzle.

10. If members of the group have committed to spending time alone with God, congratulate them and encourage them to take their commitment one step further and begin journaling. Review *Journaling 101* prior to your group meeting so that you are familiar with what it contains.

Sharing

12. It is important to return to the *Circles of Life* often, both to encourage the group to follow through on their commitments as well as to foster growth toward new commitments. Encourage the group this week to consider reaching out to their non-Christian friends, family, and acquaintances. Remind

everyone that our responsibility is to share Jesus with others, but it is the Holy Spirit's responsibility to convict souls and bring forth change.

13. Encourage group members to consider developing their salvation story as a tool for sharing their faith with others. Begin the process during your group time and encourage the group to complete the exercise at home. As leader, you should review the "Tips" section of *Telling Your Story* yourself in advance and be ready to share your ideas about this process with the group.

14. Encourage group members to think about when they are shepherding another person in Christ. This could be simply following through on inviting someone to church or reaching out to them in Christ's love. Then have everyone answer the question "WHEN are you shepherding another person in Christ?" on the *Personal Health Plan*.

Session Seven The Prostitute

Growing

This session covers Revelation 17, 18 and 21. Reading the entire selection aloud may be time-consuming so we recommend that you ask the group to read these passages at home before coming to the group.

3. Babylon may point to a particular empire or nation, current or yet to come—it's difficult to tell. But certainly Babylon represents the evil world system allied against God, as well as any government that oppresses God's people for their faith.

   Babylon allies herself with the beast, the antichrist, although in 17:16 he betrays her. She kills believers (17:6). She seduces both leaders and ordinary people to adultery with her. In the Old Testament, the prophets often compare the worship of false gods to adultery (Ezek. 16; Hosea 2), and certainly Rome tried to seduce believers into worshiping Roman gods rather than Christ. Roman power also seduced people into greed (which Paul says is idolatry, Eph. 5:5) and sexual immorality. To compromise our commitment to Christ by pursuing money, sex, power, or anything else more than we pursue him is to commit spiritual adultery.

4. The kings give all their authority to the beast, so this is essentially a war between the forces of the beast and the Lamb. Between the forces of antichrist and Christ. The Lamb triumphs because he is the rightful Lord and King. With him are his faithful followers. The prostitute world system, which has bet on the wrong side, is betrayed and destroyed.

5. This glimpse into God's absolute sovereignty over what happens in the world can be both reassuring (because he has all power, and we can trust him to use it wisely and justly) and disturbing (because many people question how

137

a good God could allow evil). Somehow, it is ultimately good to let evil have temporary power, because this reveals who are and are not Christ's faithful followers.

6. She is destroyed by God's judgment, but there's a sense that she brings her "plagues" on herself (18:8). Only the kings of the earth lament.

7. The unbelieving world is on a path to destruction. We should place our faith in the Lord, who will reign forever. The wages of sin is death; the perseverance of faith in God results in everlasting life. It's worthwhile to look at the evidence of the way we spend our time, our money, and our mental energy to see where our faith is really based.

Developing

8. Review the *Spiritual Gifts Inventory* with the group. Affirm those who have served the group or plugged into a ministry and encourage those who have not that it's never too late. If you have people still struggling with identifying their gifts, encourage them to talk to people who know them well. You might want to share what you've seen in them as well.

Session Eight Hope

Growing

This session covers Revelation 21–22. Reading the entire selection aloud may be time-consuming so we recommend that you ask the group to read these passages at home before coming to the group.

3. Genesis began with God's creation, and Revelation ends with his re-creation of a heaven and earth. This is the restoration of all things as they were intended to be before the fall of humanity. All the sinners of all the ages, both demons and humans, are in the lake of fire (20:7–15). The new city has no temple, because the Lord God Almighty and the Lamb are its temple. God is fully present with his people, and suffering is over for good. Some group members may be most moved by the end of tears, others by the intimacy with God.

4. Group members may notice a variety of things, such as the city's beauty (jewels were the ultimate beauty in John's day) and the glory of God so bright that night is banished.

6. This is a place of abundant life, of abundant and neverending fruit, of healing for all the nations.

8. Talk about what it feels like to be thirsty. Relate this to the need for that thirst to be quenched. This is what it means to need Christ and his salvation.

   Revelation ends with an invitation to those who are thirsty to come and drink from the water of life. The water of life symbolizes the continual flow of eternal life from God to heaven's inhabitants.

Sharing

11. Allow one or two group members to share for a few minutes a testimony about how they helped someone connect in Christian community or shared Jesus with an unbelieving friend or relative.

DEEPENING LIFE TOGETHER SERIES

Deepening Life Together is a series of Bible studies that offers small groups an opportunity to explore biblical subjects in several categories: books of the Bible (*Acts, Romans, John, Ephesians, Revelation*), theology (*Promises of God, Parables*), and spiritual disciplines (*Prayers of Jesus*).

A *Deepening Life Together* Video Teaching DVD companion is available for each study in the series. For each study session, the DVD contains a lesson taught by a master teacher backed by scholars giving their perspective on the subject.

Every study includes activities based on five biblical purposes of the church: Connecting, Growing, Developing, Sharing, and Surrendering. These studies will help your group deepen your walk with God while you discover what he has created you for and how you can turn his desires into an everyday reality in your lives. Experience the transformation firsthand as you begin deepening your life together.